Bent Thumb Thinking

Graham Crossan

First published by Busybird Publishing 2017
Copyright © 2017 Graham Crossan

ISBN 978-1-925692-35-8

Graham Crossan has asserted his right under the Copyright, Designs and Patents Act 1988 to be identified as the author of this work. The information in this book is based on the author's experiences and opinions. The publisher specifically disclaims responsibility for any adverse consequences, which may result from use of the information contained herein. Permission to use information has been sought by the author. Any breaches will be rectified in further editions of the book.

All rights reserved. No part of this publication may be reproduced, stored in or introduced into a retrieval system, or transmitted in any form, or by any means (electronic, mechanical, photocopying, recording or otherwise) without the prior written permission of the author. Any person who does any unauthorised act in relation to this publication may be liable to criminal prosecution and civil claims for damages. Enquiries should be made through the publisher.

Cover image: Walter Dobrowolski
Cover design: Helen McGregor & Busybird Publishing
Layout and typesetting: Busybird Publishing

Busybird Publishing
2/118 Para Road
Montmorency, Victoria
Australia 3094
www.busybird.com.au

BTT Silver Lining Sponsors
Liz Douglas
Mark Featherby
Doug Lumley
Cain Family
Selwyn Blackstone
Burke Bond Partners

BTT Worth Your Weight in Gold Sponsors
Karl Siegling www.cadencecapital.com.au
Beverley Simpson
Gillian Lechte

BTT Shine Bright Like a Diamond Sponsors
Statewide Assets Pty Ltd www.statewide-assets.com.au
Bryan Patterson

This book is dedicated to my high school English teacher, Mr. Sutherland, or Chum, as he was affectionately called behind his back. He so generously provided a safe environment for me to stretch my imagination and explore my ideas about creative writing without the shackles of convention. In his encouraging care I first dreamed of being an author.

Contents

Foreword	i
Introduction	iii
1. A Member of the World's Smallest Minority	1
2. Fun In A Matchbox	4
3. The Cops Will Catch You	7
4. My First Traffic Fine	9
5. Arguing Mathematics with A Police Officer After Midnight	16
6. Looking for Luck in the Kalahari Desert	23
7. A TV Drama called "The Lion of…Verneukapan" Starring GC	33
8. Cows, Bulls, And a Curious Boy	38
9. A Self Portrait	46
10. Watch Out! Gravity Will Get You	49
11. Dad's Pontiac Takes A Hit	51
12. How Do You Measure a Mother's Love?	53
13. Four Mothers In my Life	60
14. Help!	64
15. Granny Finds Out From A Four-Year-Old	72
16. Men May Be Brave But Woman Are Tough	76
17. Ring, Ask, Marry – A Three-Part Adventure of the Heart	82
18. Ring, Ask, Marry – Part Two	88
19. Ring, Ask, Marry – Part Three	93

20. Marriage. A Risk Reward Analysis	99
21. In a Dark World Focus on the Light	103
22. Immature Immigration Part 1	108
23. Immature Immigration Part 2	116
24. A Porcelain Picture of Hope	129
25. The Return	131
26. We Began To Talk Again	137
27. A Job Interview That Started A Beautiful Relationship	141
28. A Grandson's Most Ingenious Excuse Ever	146
29. Adult Immigration	149
30. The Worst Kind Of Bully	155
Postscript	161
MND Victoria	165
Acknowledgements	167
Supporters of BTT	169

Foreword

Some people live such an inspiring life that we can't help but catch something from them. It comes through the overflow of all that they do and say. Some people have extraordinary adversity yet live with such optimism and hope that everyone around them is encouraged. Graham is both of these.

I first met Graham at church and immediately found a unique connection. I prefer to talk about meaningful things and I found a kindred spirit in Graham. I don't like to waste time on small talk and Graham feels the same, especially since he doesn't have time to waste. We both go deep quickly, and our first conversation was around toxic thinking and how important it is to think healthy and speak healthy. At that time he was embarking on a negative word detox! I chose to cheer him on! We both agreed that words really matter, both the spoken word and those inner words that we dwell upon. Graham's urgent drive toward every form of health was because MND was making a charge on his body.

I travel extensively sharing stories of hope, courage and practical help. I have made a career through sharing motivational words that uplift, encourage and inspire. I share stories of people who have struggled and overcome and Graham is a mighty overcomer and a wonderful storyteller. He has been on a journey that most of us pray we never take. That is Motor Neurone Disease! Who wants to be told they have a terminal illness that doesn't end well? Graham has been so brave in the face of adversity. He tells me he has learned not to fear adversity because "the challenges are there to mould us, not diminish us".

When Graham began writing his thoughts down, they resonated with many. His blog went from 0 to 8000 views in under 18 months, with readers from around the world. Graham's messages are always upbeat, humorous and broadly appealing. He says, "You don't have to be perfect to have a good life" and he's learned many lessons that benefit us all. I have really enjoyed reading my friend Graham's take on life and I know that you will too.

Blessings,

Lisa

> "He writes his stories to connect and encourage. They are about family, culture, and growing up. Graham describes this book as one with a hidden hero. It's not him, but life, doing what it needs to. He just happened to be there at the time."
>
> **Lisa McInnes-Smith CSP, CPAE**
> **Best-selling Author,**
> **Inspirational Speaker and friend!**

Introduction

I've heard it said that most people learn by their own mistakes, but smart people learn by other people's mistakes.

The category I fit into is certainly not the second one, as this collection of stories will illustrate quite conclusively.

But I am comforted by the thought that there is, in fact, a third group – those people who don't learn at all.

This book is an invitation to join the "smart people". By reading about my mistakes, my naïveté and my complete unwillingness in my younger years to think things through, you may avoid some of the pain and anguish I experienced.

On the other hand, this may be too late to save you, but will reassure you that you are not alone in making decisions that seemed quite good at the time, but a lot less so in hindsight. At least we have the option of learning from them.

In reality, along the way I acquired a life companion called Gaynor, two children who have been the occasional undoing, but eventually the making of me, and friendships I cherish dearly.

So this book is a map of my road trip through 70 years of living. On 3 continents, in 3 countries and 7 cities. There's also the travel – on business and on holidays – that have all made for a life filled with moments of laughter and learning. It's been a rich and rewarding life.

> "Success is not final, failure is not fatal: it is the courage to continue that counts."
> Winston Churchill

1

A Member of the World's Smallest Minority

Fortunately, or unfortunately, depending on how you view this, I've been part of one of the most neglected and ignored minority groups on the planet. Not only that, but it's a "different-ness" I was born with and just could not hide.

In all my days I've only ever met two other people in the same minority group as me – people born with eleven fingers. That's right! Not ten, like normal people. Eleven! On my left hand were two thumbs, neither of which was quite up to scratch by conventional standards. Both pointed very much towards the right. In fact, the two formed a very convincing capital "F".

As a baby I presume there was great parental concern, followed by much deliberation about what to do with this abnormality. The outcome was that the lower "–" of the "F" was surgically removed, leaving me with a perfectly serviceable, but very imperfect bent thumb, and a five centimetre scar.

As I grew up this "abnormality" was occasionally inconvenient, periodically painful and often a source of entertainment and amusement. Even now, young boys find it fascinating – they're naturally intrigued by weird things. Young girls, on the other hand, are often mildly grossed out, because it looks bizarre. For the most part, my bent thumb has been ignored – by other people and by me. My wife, for example, didn't notice it for the first year we knew each other.

Along the way, it did take some mental and emotional gymnastics to come to terms with the reality of how I am physically. On the positive side, I've lived all my life with my bent thumb. We're best friends. Inseparable! It's been a twenty-four seven relationship we've had since I can remember. So there's a familiarity – a bond. We've been through so much together.

Surprisingly, it's never been a source of embarrassment. As a matter of fact, my life has been a little richer for it. As a child and teenager I collected a string of funny stories about it, like boasting that I was the first kid in my class able to count to eleven, that as a child I sucked my thumb so much the bone melted and sagged, as well as a dozen other stories about exactly how it came to be bent.

The truth is we're all unique. We each look different, think differently, respond differently. You may be short, or tall. You may be quiet, or loud. You may be good at sport, or blessed with dancing feet. You may be a good singer, or a good smiler.

You may be good at maths or a great cook. The way I see it, diversity is cause for celebration.

What I do know is that by being born with eleven fingers, I was forced to learn how to deal with my difference.

I've also learned that most people are so busy focusing on themselves that they're not looking at you – not nearly as much as you might imagine. And that immediately makes life easier.

Are you a member of a smaller minority group? Let me know.

2

Fun In A Matchbox

When I was four years old we lived in a block of flats. In front was a huge grass common where we rode bikes, kicked balls and did all the things children did to have fun.

With the Second World War recently ended, the birth rate had accelerated.

There were kids everywhere, and I was one of them. Our ages ranged from three to ten or eleven.

All the boys I played with were fascinated with my bent thumb. No-one else had one, or had even seen anything like it before.

One of the older boys, being among the first to notice it, came up to me quietly one school holiday morning and said: "We can have fun with your thumb."

I was only four and he was about nine, so I was going along with whatever he said.

"Look what I've made," he continued. Out of his pocket he pulled a matchbox that looked perfectly normal.

"Watch this," he said, and proceeded to slide the box open. Inside was a small bed of cotton wool stained bright red – presumably with ink.

"Give me your thumb," the boy said, and I held out my left hand. He grabbed my thumb and slid it under the box and into a hole he'd cut. He pushed it up and there it was, looking quite gruesome and macabre, inside the matchbox.

He giggled in delight and I smiled in bewilderment, not yet aware of what he had in mind to do with this creation.

"Come, let's go show someone." He took me, with the closed matchbox still on my thumb, and walked over to where a group of mums with tiny babies were sitting on a bench.

"Aunty, aunty, look at this," my raconteur friend said, waving my hand at these unsuspecting ladies.

They looked at him and he looked at the matchbox.

"This boy's broken his thumb. We need an ambulance!"

Then, with the full attention of the mums, he slid the cover back and revealed the spectacle – bent thumb with blood all around.

Their instant response was horror, with squeals of "Oh no" and "you poor darling".

But that only lasted a few seconds before one of the mums looked at me, realised I was showing no sign of pain, and said: "Wait a minute! Why's it in a matchbox?"

That was warning enough, so I was hurried away by my friend to scare some teenage girls. They were scared, but the boys he showed weren't, being more interested in the mechanics – "what happened to your thumb", "was it always like that?", and always "could I have a go at making it straighten".

For a few weeks my thumb had celebrity status. Not me, just my thumb. The kids weren't interested in me, as a person, only as the keeper of the thumb.

It was even given a nickname: The Tok tokkie thumb.

Tok tokkie is a type of beetle that frequents southern Africa. What it had to do with my bent thumb I never did find out, but it was fun while it lasted. I think!

I do know that it prepared me for a life of accepting that I am different. Not better, not worse, just different. And isn't it good that each of us is unique. What a boring world it would be if we weren't.

Port Elizabeth, South Africa
Some time in 1949

3

The Cops Will Catch You

While at university I lived in a boarding house with about fifty other young men. It was a very social environment, with late night conversations that covered – and, we believed, solved – most of the serious issues of the day.

At one point during this time, a spate of petty thefts was reported. Clothing, cash and other small items disappeared. The police were called in, who in turn called in each student for finger printing.

Down at the station we lined up and, one by one, had each finger rolled on an ink pad and then on a page of paper with our details written on it.

There was apparently a strict sequence the police officer followed, and he had obviously done this many times before because his processing was almost automatic.

When it got to my turn, he glanced up only momentarily to say: "Right hand!" I stuck out my right hand and he grabbed the thumb first. Ink, then paper. Pinky – ink, then paper. And so it went, until he had all the digits recorded.

Bent Thumb Thinking

"Left hand!" I stuck out my left hand and he grabbed the thumb.

"What's this?" asked the police officer, who'd been working in a kind of hypnotic state. He lifted my left hand up to his eye level and stared at my bent thumb, which he was still clasping tightly.

I said nothing. What was there to say?

After a brief but close examination of the subject matter, he looked into my eyes and spoke. Only seven words, but they conveyed a powerful and compelling message.

"Don't go into crime. We'll catch you."

Then he returned to his hypnotic state and completed the task. I left, considering his comment and deciding to take his advice.

A bent thumb, yes. But it would never be crooked.

                                          Grahamstown, South Africa.
                                                   Some time in 1966

4

My First Traffic Fine

Growing up is never easy, but for young men it can be a time of many trials. You want, even demand your independence, but life is full of circumstances that are new and unrehearsed. The majority of young men do their best to navigate these circumstances without asking for help, and muddle through. The experience I had in this story shows that parental support is a great advantage, although not in a way you may expect.

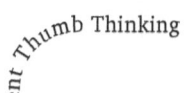

My First Traffic Fine – A Serious Case Of Confusion

How excited were you about your first car? I was, among other emotions – one of which was relief.

You see, I'd been on a three month campaign to get mine, so when it finally happened, I was very excited, but relief played a strong part.

The campaign was a propaganda program to convince my dad to buy me a car. The fact that it took that much time gives you a fair indication of how he felt at the start. But, like a three-year-old who wants an ice cream and won't give up until they have it, I persisted.

The difficulty was that every part of my campaign was conducted via long-distance phone calls that I had to pay for in twenty cent coins, and each call cost me a pocketful. I was on compulsory national service far from home.

At a certain point the conversation went a bit like this.

"But Dad, I'll work for you for as long as it takes to pay you back. I promise!"

"I don't think you know how much it costs to buy a car, or run it."

"Please, Dad. I'll work for a whole year if I have to."

There was a long pause, in which I heard the beeps indicating that my money was running out.

"I…I…I'm putting more coins in."

The familiar sound of the system registering that I had another three minutes was like music to me.

"Dad? Are you still there, Dad?"

"I'm here."

"Pleeaaaase."

Another pause.

"I've looked at a few used cars and found some options."

"You mean…?"

"Well, what do you think about owning a…?"

Dad went through a list of four or five car names, none of which exactly "revved my engine". They all sounded incredibly boring to a gung-ho eighteen-year-old, so I didn't consent to any them.

Two weekends later I hitchhiked the seven hundred kilometres home, and there it was – the mystery car! Yes, you can see it in the picture. Nothing flashy. Not a sports car. Certainly not one of the cars I'd ever aspired to own. But it was a car, and once my dad handed me the keys it was mine.

I know, you're reading this and thinking, *Yeah, but he had hours and hours of hard labour ahead of him to pay for it.* You're right, but I also had my whole life ahead, and thousands of kilometres of road to explore, so I was ecstatic.

About six months after I took ownership my military service ended and life turned sweet again. I had a temporary job, I had a car and I had time on my hands. So I did a lot of driving around.

One beautiful day, with not a cloud in the sky, I was travelling sedately along Seventeenth Avenue, which connected two suburbs by way of several kilometres of road with no houses or other buildings around. It was a place where many drivers were tempted to speed, so the local police often set traps to catch these law breakers.

On this day I was not speeding. In fact, I was ambling along in third gear. Third gear was also top gear in my 1954 Austin A50.

Life was good, or so it seemed, until a police officer stepped out from behind a bush and flagged me down.

I pulled over to the side of the road and stopped where the officer was indicating. He sauntered over and smiled. It was not a friendly smile, but more of a satisfied one, as if he was pleased with himself.

"Doing a road safety check. Need you to put your headlights on."

I did. He walked to the front of the car and checked the lights.

"Low beam now."

I did. He moved to the driver's side of the car.

"Hooter."

I pressed the hooter and prayed, because I knew it only worked intermittently, and played different notes when I went over a bump.

Miraculously it emitted a sound. It was a strange sound that was a little like a yodel. I hoped it was sufficient.

"Wipers."

Relieved that he'd passed the hooter, I flicked the wiper switch, but nothing happened.

"Wipers," he repeated, but this time more forcibly.

Again I flicked the wiper switch, but again nothing happened. My pulse rate climbed a few notches. I knew I was in trouble.

The cop smiled, pulled out his book and proceeded to write out a traffic infringement notice – a ticket, as we called it. He handed it to me.

Then he walked to the rear of the car.

"Place your foot on the brake."

I did.

"Last thing, indicators. Left turn!"

My Austin A50 had those crazy little arms that came out of the side pillar. Modern cars don't have them for one very good reason – they hardly ever worked. BUT…Austin, in their wisdom, had also fitted indicator lights, which were much more reliable. They worked about fifty percent of the time.

The officer sidled up to the driver's window and switched on his supercilious smile again.

"Indicators not operational."

He again pulled out his book and wrote out another ticket. Handing it to me he said, in a flat, Eastern Province accent:

"You betta git yor core fixed, 'cos we'll kitch you aagin."

I nodded and closed the window. This was not a part of car ownership I'd given any thought to. This was not freedom and independence. This was the opposite.

That evening, at the dinner table, I broke the news to the family. Mum and sister were sympathetic. Dad was outraged. He had that reaction to any officious action by the authorities.

"You're not paying those fines!"

I was in conflict. Part of me was feeling like, "Yes! Go Dad!" The other part was more rational, realising that if I'd done the crime, I should do the time.

"Those idiots should put their energy into catching the real bad guys, not harassing young drivers in their first cars."

The upshot was that I didn't pay, but went to court to contest the charges. My legal council was…you've guessed it! Dad. His advice was not particularly objective, but he was supportive, and what more can a young man ask of his father.

We sat through several cases before the clerk of the court read out my first fine. I was summoned to stand before the magistrate – a man who had an air of authority I'd never witnessed before. He wasn't loud or pompous, but everyone in that courtroom knew who was boss.

"How do you plead, young man?"

"Well, guilty, your honour."

"Uh huh! And do you have anything to say?"

In South African law at that time, a guilty plea allowed you the opportunity to state your case. This case was in regard to the wipers.

"Um, well, my car is very old, your honour, and the windscreen wipers were working the last time it rained. They work through an electric fuse, and the fuse must have blown. I have a whole box of them in the glove box, so whenever one blows, I just fit a new one. And that day was sunny."

There was silence.

"Is that all you want to say?" The magistrate peered at me over his reading glasses.

"Um, yes, your honour."

"Hmmm! This is your first car?"

"Yes, your honour."

"Are you a student?"

"Yes, your honour."

"OK. You were driving an un-roadworthy car, so I have to punish you. But I'm going to halve the fine, because if you're a student you probably need the money more than we do. Pay the clerk of the court."

I'd been dismissed, so I walked over to the clerk and paid the reduced amount. My dad was beside me, all smiles. He felt vindicated for advising me to contest the fine. We sat down again, expecting the very next case to me my second ticket.

It wasn't. Nor was the next one. My dad nudged me, beaming with glee.

"They've lost the other ticket. We can go."

I wasn't so sure. In my pocket was the second fine, so it appeared to me that I would be responsible for any consequences if we left too soon. So I shook my head.

As each new case went through before the court my dad's vigour increased. He insisted we leave.

"Come on. If it was going to come up it would have happened already."

My heart was pounding. What do you do when your parent is telling you one thing, but your common sense is saying the opposite?

"Graham! Let's go!"

At this point there was a loud banging from the magistrate's desk. He was incensed by the din my father was making.

"The gentleman in the navy blue jacket! If you don't shut up immediately, I'll have you up here on a charge of contempt of court!"

My dad looked down at his jacket, then around at the magistrate to confirm that he was the subject of the tirade.

It was a weird moment! Me in court, but my father being admonished. I'd never experienced that before.

We sat there chastened, wondering what would happen. Within minutes my name was read out by the clerk and I retook the dock.

Over his glasses the magistrate peered at me.

"You're the young man who was up here before, weren't you?" he asked.

I nodded.

He looked down at the papers on his desk. Then he spoke to the clerk.

"I want to see the previous ticket and this one."

The clerk shuffled some papers and handed two sheets up to the magistrate, who studied them for a moment before addressing me.

"Hmmm! How do you plead this time?"

"Guilty, your honour."

"What do you have to say?"

"Um, my car is old and…"

"Yes, yes. I remember."

"Your honour, I explained about the windscreen wipers…"

"I remember. Go on."

"The indicators work on the same fuse."

"What!"

He removed his glasses, leaned forward, and said something I've always held as a clear indication that the law can be administered with a sense of humanity and justice.

"Young man, you've got a very confused motor car."

He smiled, liking his pun, and sat back, relaxed.

"You've already paid for that fuse. No further fine will be imposed."

Dad and I walked out of that courtroom having learned a few things. Magistrates can have a sense of humour. Making a row in court can land you in trouble. And parents, with the best will in the world, can get it wrong.

The biggest lesson for me was that my misdemeanours – in the form of traffic fines – were my responsibility, not my dad's.

 "Wonderful to catch up on your illuminating stories, Graham. You certainly show us how we continue to learn from lessons in life!"

– Libby Chiselett

5

Arguing Mathematics with A Police Officer After Midnight

When we were young we were all told to do our homework. That it would pay off in the long run.

But at the time most of us doubted the long term benefits, thinking tomorrow at school was the only occasion it was likely to help us. When the teacher pointed at you and asked a question you were meant to be able to answer – that was the moment you needed to know.

One dark and lonely night, in the middle of nowhere, I was pulled over by a police officer. It was worse than being back in school.

I was twenty-two and in love.

Most of my weekends were spent tearing up and down the country visiting the subject of my adoration. The travelling was all done in the dark, because I would leave work on Friday after five, and with a rebel radio station beaming out of Mozambique and hosted by a legend named Long John Bourke blaring at full decibels, and I'd arrive at my destination several hours later.

The return trip on Sunday night was always later, because I'd play chicken, daring myself to leave at the latest possible moment. I'd calculate and recalculate just how much time I needed to be at work on time in the morning.

Yes, young and impulsive is how I'd describe myself back then.

Some factors played to my advantage. For example, like so many young men, I drove as if I was indestructible. Speed was a risk worth taking. Besides, wasn't it my skill behind the wheel that would keep me from disaster? I thought so at the time.

Other advantages included no speed limits out of town, traffic that was relatively light compared with today, and my little blue and white Mini was quick. I'd done work on the cylinder head, added a sports camshaft, and done a few other modifications to improve the performance.

To aid my midnight missions, and with the aid of an older cousin, I decided to fit a pair of high-powered driving lights to the car. Cattle and donkeys occasionally roamed the roads, and in some areas I went past regular signs that said: CAREFUL KUDU. Seeing one of these horse-sized antelope on the road in the dark was best done with enough time to take appropriate action.

Fortunately my cousin Grenville was handy with anything automotive, and he worked as an inspector for the Johannesburg Roadworthy Department, which was even handier.

"I've got two lights to put on," I explained.

"Hmmm!' he reflected. "You might need a special bracket to hold two."

"But I'm going away tomorrow night, so I've got no time to buy one," I moaned.

At that age, when I wanted something, I wanted it NOW! Didn't we all?

"Well, maybe we can fit just one now and you can try it out before you go spending any money," my patient cousin suggested.

So that's what we did, but only after studying the Road Ordinance Manual he worked from every day in his job. We wanted to be sure we were doing it properly.

I drove home that evening excited by the prospect of trying the light out on my journey the next night.

Twenty-four hours ticked by and I was off, speeding along with my backside only inches from the road. I ate a huge hamburger with the lot and drank a pint of milk after the half way stop for fuel. Dexterity was another skill I took pride in, not spilling a drop or leaving a mark of fried onion or fried egg on my clothes.

I loved being in my Mini, slicing through town traffic, then winding up the tiny wheels and letting them loose as the sun set and darkness dimmed all distractions beyond the headlight beams. But that night I didn't do the test. There was too much traffic and I knew what it was like to have an oncoming car not dim their lights.

Sunday arrived. The day departed. I didn't. Well not until I was convinced that if I didn't leave immediately, my boss would be displeased with my lateness on Monday morning.

Off into the night I blasted, not aware that there was someone else on the road with whom I would cross paths and swords a few hours later.

In no time it was three in the morning. Just me, the Mini and Long Johnny B alone under the brilliant starlit African sky. No other cars on the road. No cares in the world.

This was the time to try out my new light. I was excited.

Making sure there were no cars ahead or behind me, I stretched down and flipped the new light switch. Instantly the world before me came alive. Details appeared that were invisible before.

I switched the light off, to see the difference. Then on again it went. I was ecstatic. Why had I waited so long to do this? And what would it be like with two driving lights? I could imagine that any kudu would be visible a mile away. It was like daylight!

I switched it off, the test infinitely successful.

And as I smiled and dreamed of speeding around South Africa at night, sitting behind this powerful shaft of light, the peace was shattered by the sound of a siren and the unmistakeable flash of a blue police light in my rear view mirror.

I slowed and stopped. The police car pulled up behind me. Out stepped the cop. I did the same. We both wrapped our collars around our necks to keep out the cold.

"Can I see your driver's license?" He stopped a short distance from me.

"Yes, here," I smiled, wanting to appear friendly and assured of my innocence. I held it out for him.

He took it, looked carefully at the photo, then at me, and nodded.

'You used high powered lights at a time you shouldn't," he accused.

"But I made sure there were no cars coming, officer."

And to enhance my point, I continued: "Look, there aren't any cars. Not one has come past since we stopped."

He looked up and down the road, then shrugged.

"You aren't allowed to have any auxiliary light connected to the dimming switch. It's illegal and I must fine you."

"But I haven't, officer. It's got its own switch."

"Let me see," insisted the cop, who was probably just bored with patrolling the highway this late at night. There was nothing better to do.

I showed him the switch, but he persevered.

"How many extra lights have you got?"

"One."

"That's not allowed. It's illegal. You're in trouble now."

"But…" I didn't know what to say, or do.

"You must have two," he insisted.

I knew what my cousin and I had read, but wasn't sure I should argue the toss with a cop way out here. The predicament was a little intimidating for me. I was only in my early twenties, living in a police state.

Then, from out of my mouth came a statement that was more like a challenge.

"The Road Ordinance Manual doesn't say that," I insisted.

This rocked the police officer back. What did this snotty nosed young upstart know about the road ordinances? He shook his head. I didn't know whether it was disbelief that I could have so much audacity, or that he didn't agree with my statement.

"No, no, no, man," he proclaimed.

"Yes, it's true," I fought back.

"No, man, that's not correct. I'm going to fine you."

"For WHAT?"

My beautiful drive home was going horribly wrong.

"Officer, have you got a copy of the Road Ordinance Manual?" I asked. "I'll show you."

Very slowly and reluctantly the cop walked back to his vehicle and returned with the manual. He handed it to me, probably hoping to have called my bluff. But I remembered the section and article number, and immediately turned to it.

By torchlight we read the article aloud. In unison. That is, until we got to this:

…must be mounted equidistant from the centre of the bumper…

"There's your mistake," enthused the policeman.

"What?" I protested.

"Equidistant," he gloated. "Your light is not mounted equidistant from the centre of the bumper."

By now we were standing in front of the Mini, staring down at the single light that looked so innocuous and innocent.

"But officer, technically it is," I argued.

"Is what?" he asked.

"Equidistant," I answered.

There was a long silence. We each considered our battle plan and the next move. I resorted to mathematics, a subject perfect for baffling the unsuspecting.

"If you only have one light, equidistant is in the middle," I offered.

"No, no, no, man. That's not correct."

"It is, sir. It's like if you divide one by one you get one."

This appeared to baffle him. He took a deep breath and let it out slowly as he considered his options. The breath came out in a stream of steam. It was freezing out there.

I had the fleeting feeling I was winning the mental battle.

Then the police officer grabbed his manual, strode off to his vehicle, and returned with a ticket book. The winning feeling evaporated. I wondered what he'd decided.

"I'm going to give you an ticket. It's a serious offence, this light, if it's wrong."

My heart sank.

"But I'm writing on the bottom of the ticket that if you get it inspected at the Johannesburg Roadworthy Department before eight-thirty today, this fine will be null and void. They can decide. You understand?"

I nodded, but not too enthusiastically, because I didn't want to give away any sign of the glee I was feeling.

"Thank you, officer. I'll go straight there and wait till it opens. It's on my way to work."

And that's what I did. I arrived at six, so was first in the queue by about an hour. When the gates opened, I went looking for Grenville. He was an inspector, and already knew that my driving light was correctly mounted.

"Morning Graham," he greeted me. "How did the light work?"

My reply was to hand him the ticket. After reading it my cousin smiled a broad smile.

"So you had some fun and games on your journey. And the

cop's underlined the one word several times – EQUIDISTANT. What's that all about?"

I explained the argument and we both laughed.

"Don't worry about the fine," reassured Grenville, "I'll take care of that. But we'd better mount the two very soon. Or you'll be stopped again. Next time you might lose the argument, 'cos I reckon the ordinance does imply that there should be more than one light."

The next weekend my Mini had some work done on it. Two lights were mounted according to the manual. And great care was taken to measure the distance from the centre of the bumper before drilling the holes.

I did my homework well again this time. There was no knowing when another mathematical debate might take place in the middle of nowhere.

6

Looking for Luck in the Kalahari Desert

You know what it's like when you've had a tough week at the end of a tough month at the end of a tough year. You need a break. Badly!

Easter was coming up and I had some leave long overdue. So we decided, the family and I, to take off for the wide open spaces. For two weeks we were leaving behind the big smoke of Johannesburg, with its busy streets and crowds of people, to find some respite in the wilds of Africa with its dirt tracks and herds of animals.

Way out in the Kalahari desert is a game park of rare beauty.

This place has red earth sparsely covered in patches of long, golden grass, with occasional acacia trees growing along the banks of two converging dry river beds. It also sports some of the most spectacular antelope, lions, leopards, cheetahs, hyenas and a multitude of other fauna, that I've ever seen.

It's a vast and wild tract of land where life is sustained through constant vigilance and a determination to be among the stronger, rather than the weaker, of your species. It's a constant struggle to survive. Each and every day this natural process takes place, as regularly as the sun rises and the sun sets.

The most appealing aspect of this game park turned out to be the fact that in a day's driving only two or three other vehicles would pass us by. So to recharge the batteries, regain some composure, and reconnect with the 'real' world, this was the place to be.

However, the Kalahari Gemsbok Park had something else in store for us – something more rare than all the wildlife in Africa.

Oh, we watched a cheetah mother teaching her two very apprehensive young cubs to hunt, and we had a lioness suddenly stride out of the grass only metres away when we were foolishly standing outside our Land Rover. We saw the most breathtaking spectacles of wildebeest, hartebeest, bontebok and springbok – herds of thousands moving through the dry river beds in the soft early morning light. It was wonderful. This was nature in Cinemascope, Technicolour and Surround Sound.

But the highlight of the holiday was when our Land Rover broke down.

Strange as that might sound, it's true! At the end of our third day we were making our way back to the camp where our caravan was parked. With five kilometres to go there was an almighty bang in the engine, followed by a clanging sound that rose and fell in harmony with the revs.

It was certainly not a comforting sound, especially with sunset just half an hour away and the thought that dusk was possibly feeding time for all those carnivores out there.

We had to get to the camp. So with great care and caution I nursed the Landie along the remaining riverbed road, up a steepish rise, along a narrow track, through the huge security gates, and into the safety of the camp. Phew!

On arrival our first stop was the park rangers' office, where I received a curt response to my plea for help.

"Follow the track south. In 15 kilometres you'll go past a sign that says 'Welcome'. Just past that you'll come to a T-junction. Stop. Look right. There's big peppercorn trees. Under the trees is the old man. He'll help you."

It sounded like instructions scratched on the wall of Aladdin's cave. Fairytale stuff. However, the next morning I set out with the family to find this peppercorn tree man.

We clunked cautiously down the track leading out of the game reserve. It was slow going. The clunking inside the engine made my stomach churn. After almost exactly 15 kilometres we saw a faded sign hanging on a pole beside the road saying "Welcome to the Kalahari Gemsbok Park – Home of the Black Maned Lion".

On we crept until we reached the T-junction and, sure enough, on the right was a grove of giant peppercorn trees. But where was the old man? I turned in and drove cautiously forward. Way back there, in the shadows of those monstrous trees that had somehow survived the perpetual drought, was a petrol pump, and further back, almost undetectable, was a large corrugated iron workshop.

As we laboured up to the shed a short, powerfully built man in his late sixties walked out, wearing the cleanest, whitest overalls I'd ever seen. On his head – way out in the Kalahari desert – was a sailor's cap. He smiled a quiet and friendly smile and greeted us with a raised hand. This was the old man. He was not a character in an ancient story, but reassuringly real.

I stopped the Land Rover and stepped out. In Afrikaans, which I was not proficient at, I introduced myself and started explaining my problem. His response was to raise his hand, assuring me that he'd heard the clanging. Then he changed his focus and began to reassure my wife, Gaynor, and the children.

In his mother tongue he spoke to her: "Mevrou mustn't worry," he said calmingly. "Makes no difference what the problem is, I can help. Mustn't worry." Then he turned to me and, smiling, said: "Just a moment, meneer."

Out here men, it seemed, were required to be steadfast and resolute, the rock and the strength for their family. Showing anxiety was not the done thing if you were a man.

He walked unhurriedly into the workshop, returning with the longest screwdriver I'd ever seen. "Start up, please, meneer."

I did as he asked, then moved over to where he was lifting the bonnet.

He nodded his head to me as if to say, "we both know about these things," then turned away.

"Mevrou," he gestured for Gaynor to come to where he was standing. She moved closer, followed inquisitively by the two children. " Mevrou mustn't worry," he repeated in that formal tone so typical of his generation. "Jy sien, met elke ongeluk kom geluk. Maar…jy moet dit soek."

In English: "You see, with every bit of bad luck, there's always some good luck. But…a person must look for it. Come, we look."

I must explain that this conversation loses greatly in the translation. At the time I was not bowled over, believing I'd heard some deep philosophical statement. But what did amaze me was that he proceeded with great persistence over the next few hours to demonstrate the validity of this belief.

Using the oversized screwdriver like a stethoscope, he placed the pointy end on various parts of the engine and raised the handle to his ear, listening intently. At each point he smiled, raised his head, and said, not to me, but to my wife, "See, it's not the rocker arms, so that's some good luck." She nodded her silent gratitude. Then he listened further along: "Mmmm! No, it's not the…" So the examination proceeded.

This was not some fast talking city slicker ready to slap a $500 charge on the next unfortunate travellers. This was a man who took his duty seriously. He knew we were depending on him.

Finally he glanced up – this time at me. "Mmmm!" he concluded gravely. "Your problem lies in here, meneer." Then a hint of a smile formed on the corners of his mouth, and he nodded.

In order to save me some money, he instructed me to remove the fan and radiator, then to loosen the timing cover. "But only loosen it, meneer. Don't take it off!"

He loaned me his assistant, a man of diminutive stature like many of the local indigenous people. This man's name was 'Kantoor', meaning 'Office' and presumably an aspiration his parents had for him at birth.

I did as I was told. Kantoor and I worked quietly and co-operatively. When we'd finished the task the old man returned. He beckoned my wife to watch carefully as he made ready to remove the cover.

"Your bad luck's in here," he said, his brow furrowed with concern. "But your good luck is in here also. We just need to find it." He smiled. "Maybe we have to look hard, hey, but it's in here for sure."

Slowly he removed the remaining bolts and gently tilted back the cover to reveal the timing chain inside.

A series of "Hmmms" emerged, then his face lit up. "Ah ha! See here, mevrou, meneer," he said. "It's broken off. That's what made the bang. The bracket. Daar's jou ongeluk. There's your bad luck. But now.....where has it gone?"

With great care he angled the cover further back, revealing the gear at the bottom. My wife, the children and I all craned our necks to see. It was like an audience at a magician's show, trying to see the sleight of hand. Would there be the inevitable good luck, as the old man had suggested?

"Mevrou! Look!"

He whispered this in amazement to my wife, who's head was now almost under the timing cover as well. She'd never before realised what mysteries and intense dramas lay hidden under a Land Rover bonnet.

"Where?" she whispered.

"Look! See! It's lying outside. That broken bracket should have fallen down here" he pointed, "between the chain and the gear."

With a knowing shake of his grey head he contemplated the consequence.

"Now that would have made a very big mess. But look what happened! It jumped around and has fallen on the outside, so nothing is damaged. How did it do that?"

He looked up to the heavens as if in recognition of some greater power at work. In agreement we all nodded in amazement at this mechanical miracle. It was a miracle! The old man, who worked on things of this nature all day and every day, had told us it was.

The bigger miracle, on reflection, was his unswerving belief and his sense of pure and simple wonderment when he found it.

"You see! There's your good luck. We just needed to look for it."

Simplistic perhaps, but out there where life is so precarious, because there is always death lurking beyond the next sand dune, that old man needed his life to be governed by certain beliefs. Survival in such a primitive and unforgiving place calls for clear and concise thinking. Thinking that is essentially positive, no matter what problems may rear their heads, is the bedrock of life and progress.

When it was almost time to leave I asked him about the farmers in the area. I was curious about how they managed in such harsh and arid conditions.

His gentle eyes searched the far horizon before he answered. "Meneer, this is good land, as long as you have a big farm and you can find water. You know, underground water."

"I see, and do the farms around here all have plenty of water?"

He rubbed his chin and his eyes swept the horizon again, as though he was searching his memory banks to ensure he gave me an accurate answer. Every question that day was treated by him with the same earnest consideration.

"Yes. Except that place right over there." He pointed east to the other side of the dirt road that ran into the game park. From where we were standing, all I could see was scrub and sand dunes sparsely covered with grass tufts.

Then he began his final story about good and bad luck, although by now I was convinced that 'luck' as we know it, was not what he meant. In all his examples there was an underlying theme of faith and endeavour. A sense that always, in every situation, lay some divine benevolence, some choice for us to make. We could curse the problem, the bad luck, or we could press on, eyes open to the alternative, the positive.

This is what he told me: "For thirty years I watched one farmer then another farmer buy that place. Each one was sure they could make a success out of it. Ja! That was when they arrived. And they all worked hard."

He shook his head slowly, privately paging through his memories of past owners and their respective struggles.

"Nobody comes out here to the Kalahari thinking life will be easy. Oh no! They knew it would be hard. And two, maybe three years later they would be very tired, very sad. Because why? No money left. They have to sell. I even saw men cry, you know. Tough men!"

In the city it's not often one sees men cry, but out in the bush, where the men are bred strong and resilient, the sight must have meant real heartbreak.

The old man continued. "No-one ever found water. They drilled that plaas so full of holes it would have sunk if there had been water there. Never found one single drop."

He spoke these words as if he carried a heaviness inside, a sadness for all those unfulfilled dreams. Dreams he'd watched dry up in the scorching Kalahari sun.

After reflecting on this I asked: "Does no-one live there now?"

"Oh yes," he said, returning from his memories. "A young couple, even younger than you and your wife. About six years ago they drove in here. I thought they were here for repairs. It was a very old car. But they needed petrol." The old man smiled as he remembered. "They were excited, like newlyweds. You understand?"

"I asked them how long they were staying…at the game reserve. 'Meneer, we're your new neighbours. We've bought the farm across the road.'"

In the fading light of the Kalahari the old man stroked his beard, recollecting the look on their face, then he continued the story.

"You know, I felt so sorry when they pointed over there. I was hoping they were wrong."

From the old man's face it was apparent how he'd felt when those young hopefuls explained that they were adding their name to the long list of failures.

I simply nodded, believing the story to be over. My mind filled in the blanks: they'd spent their savings on the property, drilled a few holes and eventually driven away into the spectacular Kalahari sunset, never to be seen in those parts again.

But I was wrong. After a long stare across the dusty yard, the old man continued.

"Good people…very good. You know what they did! Paid me extra money – for future provisions. Told me how her brother would be coming through with a drilling rig. They said he was an expert at finding water. He'd been doing it for eleven months already."

He smiled and his ample stomach vibrated with some deep inner mirth, but no sound emerged from his mouth. "Then they said goodbye and drove off."

"The next day the brother-in-law arrived. He was driving a thirty-year-old truck pulling an ancient drilling rig. He was just as excited as the other two. I remember he also told me he was a water expert, but his equipment told me he was not. You see, in those days I still believed more in bad luck than good luck.

"Anyway, maybe three days later the young lady came to the store to buy fresh food. She was still smiling, just like that first day. I thought she was…you know, like when a woman is pregnant for the first time. She looked like she needed to tell me something.

"I asked her if everything was going well. She told me. That same afternoon when her brother-in-law arrived, they were sitting down to eat. When they were finished it was still light, so the two men thought they might as well go and look around the farm. Maybe plan for the next day.

"They climbed into the old truck and started driving. The drill was still on the back. Then ... bad luck!"

The old man shook his head gently, as if he could feel the frustration of a broken down truck.

"Meneer, mevrou, those to youngsters…they did something very clever. They were wise men. They taught me something! Even old people can learn. Even from young ones!"

My wife couldn't contain her curiosity any longer. "What happened?"

"That truck! It broke down only about two kilometres from the farmhouse. But! Those two decided: 'bad luck always hides good luck.' The one worked on the truck. That was what he knew about. And the other one decided he might as well test the drill, to see if it was still working, after all the dust and bumps on the bad roads.

"First hole! Water! Can you believe it? And so close to the house."

The old man shook his head gently and smiled. Again I was struck by his innocent acceptance. He was truly in awe, and quite comfortable that it was meant to happen.

"You see, they had their bad luck, but they didn't stop to complain. They looked for the good luck.

"When the truck started again they drove on, but it didn't go far. Only a few hundred yards. So they did the same. They hit water again! Never complained about the truck. Just went looking for some good luck hidden with the bad luck.

"Do they still live there?" I asked.

"The brother-in-law has gone now, but the young couple, they're doing very well. Got five children. They call me Oupa. Very nice family. They've been good for this district."

The conversation subsided as we all thought about the story and the concept of good luck going hand in hand with bad luck.

My personal thoughts turned to the question of what this old man's tale was really about? Was it pointing to accepting the bad things that come along, and just get on with life? Perhaps it was more a matter of accepting the reality that bad things will inevitably come along, but the way to deal with them is a choice?

I paid the old man, shook his hand, thanked him sincerely for his help and hospitality, and drove off into the red sand dunes of the Kalahari, seeing life through altered lenses.

Yes, there's not an abundance of rainfall out in the desert, but life is still there in all its richness. We need to look beyond the dryness, though, to find it.

(NB: This story is available in Afrikaans on the Bent Thumb Thinking Blog site.)

 "A remarkable story that had me captivated."
– Bryan Patterson

7

A TV Drama called "The Lion of...Verneukpan" Starring GC

Sometimes events thrust us into a role we don't feel suited to. In my early thirties I definitely didn't see myself in the role of anything too frivolous, but in this drama the joke was on me.

'The Lion Of Verneukpan' – My First Role In A Scary Movie

Working in the advertising industry meant life was never boring. It was high pressure, but there were rewards for the long hours and occasional all-nighters.

One of the most exciting parts of my job as a copywriter and creative director working primarily on automotive advertising was film shoots. As the writer of the scripts, and possibly the only one in the agency who knew the difference between a big end and a small end bearing, I went on all the car shoots. They were, for the most part, fun.

In the seventies there were no computer graphics available. There were also no miniaturised cameras or steadycam devices to help produce the amazing images we see in car commercials on TV today. So we had to be inventive in other ways.

On one particular shoot, producing all the visual material for the launch of the new look Ford Escort Mk ll, we planned a trip into the wilds of southern Africa. My friend and film director, Volker Miros, was in charge.

The concept was 'Car Choreography' and the location was a saltpan where Sir Donald Campbell unsuccessfully attempted to break the land speed record. We would use it to make the bright new cars dance in an ice dancing fashion.

The crew was huge, because we had three Ford Escorts, three models to drive them, makeup artist, wardrobe, film crew, sound crew, a helicopter, director, producer, assistants for everyone, and me. Oh, and because we'd be filming in the middle of nowhere, some three hundred kilometres north of Cape Town, all the accommodation and catering had to come along too.

So we set off early in a procession of cars and caravans, trucks and vans, that stretched back a long way. Verneukpan was our destination and we reached it in time to start setting up our makeshift home.

Each person was allocated a sleeping place and I drew the short straw, with a stretcher in the only partly enclosed annex of one of the caravans. But I was happy, deciding that fresh air and the stars above as I slept were worth the possible draftiness and exposure my bed might provide.

Night fell spectacularly over the semi-desert landscape, and we all went to sleep knowing that tomorrow would be a very long day. So when we had finished a magnificent evening meal in the huge mess tent, everyone hit the sack.

Day one was a planning and preparing day. The helicopter

and its fuel truck arrived. The drivers of the hero cars were briefed and rehearsed. The equipment was assembled and tested. Shotlists and shooting sequences were finalised. We were ready.

Another spectacular evening ended the day. Off to bed we all trickled, now reasonably familiar with where our lodgings were in the maze of accommodation.

I crawled into my sleeping bag, stared up into a sky filled with jewels that are never as bright in the city, thought about how lucky I was to live in a place where the wild open spaces still were wild and open, and fell asleep.

The chill of the morning woke me early. Brrr! I dragged on a tracksuit and hurried in the pre-dawn light to the almost deserted mess tent. With a big mug of hot tea in my hand I sat down at a table on my own.

On the other end of the tent were some of the film crew – all people I'd worked with before, but I felt the need for space while I woke completely.

After a few minutes of sipping my tea my brain had engaged and I heard someone behind me speaking.

"Hey, guys! Did you hear that carry on last night?"

The people at the table, to my surprise, nodded vigorously.

"Yeah! It was incredible."

"What? What are you talking about?" I asked.

"The noises in the camp."

"I reckon there was a lion roaming around the camp at around three this morning."

"A lion? No way," I declared, although my mind was instantly considering the possibility. This was not all that far from the Kalahari, where the famous black-maned lions ruled the world.

"Where exactly were the sounds?" I enquired.

They explained and the more details that emerged, the more I thought this was right where I'd been at that time. But, a lion in the camp? Naah!

"Nice one, guys. I don't believe it."

By then a number of other crew members had wandered in, one of whom was the sound recording engineer.

"I recorded it. Wanna hear?"

I nodded, so off he went for his recorder. He gave me the earphones but said he'd turn up the volume so we could all hear.

The sound rocked me to my core. It started low and progressed to a mighty crescendo. Then it started again. And on it went.

The thought of a full grown lion lazily ambling through the camp, and possibly right past where I was sleeping in sublime ignorance of the danger right beside me, sent a chill down my spine.

He played it again. This time I conceded.

"That's incredible! There's no way I'm sleeping in the same place tonight!"

Everyone nodded in agreement. Then the first snigger filled the silence, followed by another and another.

"What?" I asked, shrugging my shoulders and shaking my head in confusion.

Everyone was looking at me with a huge grin on their face. That progressed to raucous laughter, and it was pretty obvious that I was the joke.

"What are you all laughing at?" I quizzed.

"Don't you get it?" the sound guy said.

"Everyone in the camp was there. Even you."

"Huh? I was asleep," I explained.

"You were snoring so loud we thought it WAS a lion. So we recorded it. We didn't want you to miss out."

I laughed. It was a weak laugh, because at the age I was then the concept of laughing at one's self had not yet been learned. With a few pats on my back, everyone went off to have their breakfast.

The rest of the film shoot went well, and it did make me realise that people can laugh at the things you do without diminishing who you are. It occurred to me that less friendly people than them might just have given me a poke in the ribs and a shout to "SHUT UP".

Instead, they allowed me to be the Lion of Verneukpan for one night.

8

Cows, Bulls, And a Curious Boy

Any parent will tell you – six-year-olds are curious creatures.

By that I mean two things. For a start, their brains are like sponges, soaking up every item of information available to fill the sparsely used hard drive they were born with. But – and this is the second thing – the information they soak up has to conform to some innate 'Six-Year-Old' format or code in order to pass through their firewall and be saved.

My six-year-old son, Simon, was a case in point. His hunger for information meant our conversations were peppered with the words "what", "why", "how" and "when".

"Da-ad…um…"

It amazed me. A simple yes or no answer seldom satisfied him. But I was happy to comply. Not being a great conversationalist myself, his questions helped me speak on subjects I might not otherwise have considered. Certainly I wouldn't have thought to speak to him, or any other six-year-old about them.

At that age Simon's attention was being drawn increasingly to the subject of differences. For instance, he'd noticed that there were certain fundamental differences between boys and girls, men and women. Of course, he recognised that these disparities extended to dogs, horses, cattle and a number of other animals.

So the time was approaching for us to have a little chat. Every parent knows about 'the talk', often euphemistically referred to as the 'birds and bees' talk.

I don't believe parents just shy away from it out of embarrassment. It's more to do with an anxiety not to get it wrong. To explain in a way that will misrepresent the details of such an important topic.

Sex is also a subject often avoided until the child is a teenager, but with Simon the pressure was being applied to me by someone much younger.

How to do it right? My own experience as a child was having a book thrust into my hand, not by a father concerned to provide information, but a mother frustrated by her husband's ongoing reluctance to broach the subject.

I never read that book. A flick through the pages, and a sideways glance at the illustrations grossed me out. But I was only young. What would Simon's reaction be?

I needn't have worried, because along came George. Farmer George.

I must explain that Farmer George was a mine manager in his real life, a hunter in his fun life and a part time farmer in his spare time life.

This was the 1970s in South Africa. A different time, with different attitudes to many things, including children. Especially if your name was George, and you were a mine manager, a hunter and…all the other things I'd heard about him on the grapevine.

Rumours they were, but one of them was to do with hunting without a license, on other people's property. It's also called poaching – a taboo subject because it was, and still is, illegal.

George and I met when I was invited to spend a day on his farm. Simon came along to make it a boy's day out. The man made a lasting impression on both of us.

During the thirty-minute drive, with the three of us packed into the front seat of his F100 pickup truck, George told us how he'd always wanted to own land, and how he'd recently acquired it. Now he farmed cattle and game.

We arrived, drove to some low sheds, and George spoke briefly with the foreman and workers about the day's agenda. Then he took us for a conducted tour.

This was one proud property owner. You could hear it in his voice. He didn't boast as such, but it was obvious he was still in the honeymoon stage of being a farmer. Already George had made some adjustments.

Most important, he told me, was that he'd stocked the farm with game – springbok, hartebeest, kudu and other antelope – which could become a financial asset.

As we drove around the dirt tracks, George was focussed on only one thing – sighting his wildlife. And when he did, he performed a most curious act.

He'd raise an imaginary rifle to his shoulder, take careful aim, pull the trigger, and shout: 'BANG!' He'd even rock back from the recoil.

"What was that?" I asked the first time he did this.

"Shhhh!" he whispered, as though we were really hunting. "Can you see it? There, in the shadows under that thorn tree."

"What?" I asked, able to see several thorn trees, but unable to recognise any shape in the shadows.

"There!" Simon could see what I couldn't.

"My big Kudu bull. He's my pride and joy."

"Do you ever shoot here, you know, with a gun?" I asked innocently.

"Of course not! These are mine!"

As we drove, admiring animals and shooting several beauties with that imaginary rifle that never missed, I got to know a good deal more about George.

He was full of life. He was great company. He was energetic. He loved the land. And he loved hunting – other people's game. George was a straight shooter. There was no subtlety, no room for misunderstanding. What you saw, or heard, is what you got.

I wondered how much of this made sense to Simon, but felt sure he'd be comfortable with one aspect. Ask a simple question, get a simple answer.

By the time we got back to the farm sheds the cattle herds had been rounded up and were milling around in a large fenced enclosure. The next hour, George explained, was going to be engaged in inoculating these animals.

We agreed to watch. Simon, curious about what was about to happen, perched himself right beside me, with his feet on the bottom bar of the sturdy wooden fence, his mouth and my left ear in perfect position for the stream of questions that were certain to come.

Sure enough, as individual animals were herded into a narrow race, then stopped at the gate so the injection could be administered, he started. What, why, how?

He kept watching and listening. After an inoculation, as each animal was released, an instruction was shouted out regarding the next animal.

"Koei!"

This meant the next beast coming down the race was a cow.

"Bull!"

We could see a switching of syringes as well as the bottle from which the dosage was drawn, when "bull" was called out.

It took a while for one particular mystery to form in Simon's mind. As closely as he watched, he could not work out one important aspect of the process.

"Da-ad!"

"Yes, Simon."

"How do they know when it's a bull and when it's a cow?"

A perfectly reasonable question asked in the best possible place – the farmyard.

I did what many people will judge as taking the coward's way out, but I think it was inspired, especially considering what transpired.

"The best person to ask is George. He's the farmer. I think you should ask him."

Somewhat reluctantly Simon followed me as we moved over to where the workers were standing.

As George looked toward us, I passed the buck.

"George, Simon's got a question he wants to ask you."

"What d'you want to know, booitjie?"

George smiled gently, perhaps to encourage Simon to ask any question he liked. It was social engagement on a very personal level.

Simon looked at me, then turned back to George and asked the question.

"How do you know when it's a bull and when it's a cow?"

George didn't blink. He didn't bluster. He just answered.

"Easy. Come. I'll show you."

The two, my six-year-old son, whom I adored, and a fifty-year-old farmer we'd only met a few hours earlier, turned together to where the animals were still being processed and the lesson began.

George, equipped with a metre long stick, answered the question with a question.

"Look here, Simon. You see this?" He pointed to the udder of the animal being inoculated.

"Ye-yes," answered Simon, possibly wondering if this was a trick question.

"Do you know what it is?" He looked directly at Simon.

"Ummm!"

"That's right. It's the udder, where the cow's milk comes from."

Having answered the first question himself, George continued the conversation.

"You see these?" He used the stick to point. "Do you know what they are?"

Simon, with all that six-year-old inquisitiveness focussed on what George was pointing at, shook his head. He looked at George, knowing he was about to find out.

"Teats. The milk comes out of them. A calf sucks on them, and we get milk for breakfast from them."

This was information Simon accepted.

"How many teats can you see?"

Now we were getting into a subject Simon enjoyed – arithmetic. Bending down to get a clear view, he counted.

"One, two, three…FOUR!"

"Correct."

It didn't show on his face, but I was sure Simon was smiling inside. He was following George's process every step so far.

"So now we're going to check. Let's have a look at this one."

George and Simon stood together while the next few animals entered the race, had their shot, and exited to our left. With each one George asked Simon to check the udder and count the teats.

Step One was completed as a simple arithmetic exercise. Step Two was along similar mathematical lines. In order to facilitate this, George gave the foreman some unintelligible instructions, and waited for the next animal to reach the front.

"What's this, Simon?" The farmer, as patient as every successful farmer has to be, turned to watch Simon go through the identification process. One udder, four teats.

"It's a cow!" Simon's face was triumphant.

"Correct. Now look over here."

George moved to his right, until he was in line with the rear of the cow, and lifted the tail with his hand. High.

Simon was spellbound, anticipating some new piece of information that he could add to the jigsaw puzzle being assembled in his head.

Bent Thumb Thinking

"What do you see?" A very direct question, especially when you're looking at the sight we were confronted with.

Simon's face was blank, although I have no doubt his mind was in hyperdrive.

"Look. Two holes," explained George, pointing to the exhibit just as any good teacher would. "Remember for later."

By then his instructions had been carried out. The cow exited and the next beast came snorting and stamping down the race. Once it was in position, George pointed.

"What's that there?"

Simon investigated.

"An udder," he declared confidently. George nodded.

"OK. How many teats?"

Simon looked at George, then back to where the stick was pointing. His facial expression changed to a frown.

"None."

His eyes were wide and his voice uncertain, as if he'd discovered something that didn't add up. George reassured him with a nod.

"Correct. So now what? You can't get any milk there."

With the most serious face, Simon conceded this point.

"But watch here, Simon," continued George, pointing at something hanging in front of the 'udder' in question. "See this? It's a pipe."

Simon looked and nodded. George moved to the rear of the animal and lifted its tail.

"Look. How many holes, Simon?"

Simon studied that area carefully and thoroughly, but could only come up with a count of one.

"That's because it's a bull."

The conversation continued. George explained in simple, mechanical terms what each piece of animal equipment was used for and the outcome. It was inspired – binary code for six-year-old boys. Ones and zeroes that work in precise sequences, especially when it comes to how calves are created. Any other sequence doesn't work, said George.

Simon absorbed it all.

He'd only asked that one question all visit, but the answer satisfied his curiosity completely. So completely, in fact, that when we arrived back at Grandma's house, Simon couldn't contain himself. Rushing in, he confronted her with the second big question for the day:

"Granny, do you know the difference between a bull and a cow?"

Grandma, who was quite sure she knew the answer, learned details she was previously unaware of – like pipes and udders with no teats.

The saying goes that 'when the student is ready, the teacher will appear'. The meeting of Simon and George, in that case, was meant to be. I was also a student that day.

It took some time before Simon saw the funny side of the story.

 "Great story. I could have used your account of a father-son talk with my boys."
   – James Parsons

9

A Self Portrait

I've always been a sentimental bloke. Even when I was young I seemed to prefer stories of struggle to tales of conquest. I was also more receptive to ballads than to other types of music.

I remember being in my thirties and hearing a Simon & Garfunkel song that went like this:

"Old friends…sit on their park bench like book ends"

And the end of the song said:

"Preserve your memories. They're all that's left you".

Rather sombre for someone as young as I was then, but the words, while they didn't mean anything to me on a personal level, resonated powerfully with me on a human level.

And here I am now, sitting on "my park bench" sifting through my memories.

What I have come to realise, in the half century since that song was a hit, is that memories are peculiar and very personal. For example, much of the paraphernalia I have around me these days would be of no interest, or value, to anyone else but me. Which means it has no monetary value whatsoever. It's all sentimental stuff.

"I (me)" S. Crossan Pass Sub A

In our younger years we've all gone into an old person's home, looked around, and shaken our heads. What we see everywhere appears to be rubbish to us. But I now know the reason.

Next to my bed is a drawing.

It's of a boy in his school uniform. At the bottom, written in clear and precise 'teacher text' are the words: "I (me)" and next to that the name "S.Crossan".

Artistically this is just a naïve child's drawing – a self-portrait of my son in his first year at school. The face is smiling, the eyes are blue, there is some detail given to the uniform, particularly the school tie. Even the pattern of the stripes is accurate.

You see, Simon was into detail at that age.

It's not particularly different to the drawings of any child in their first year of school. That is, if you look at it through eyes that are not this father's eyes. Therein lies the clue to answer this question:

Why would I, after 40 years, still cherish this brown paper drawing?

You could guess that it's simply for sentimental reasons, and you would be correct to some extent. But there is something quite special about it that connects father and son in a subconscious sense. That "something" makes the drawing even more precious to me than to Simon's mum.

In that classroom on the slopes of Table Mountain, Simon must have had a momentary lapse in concentration as he toiled to two-dimensionalise himself.

What I saw was a drawing of Simon with two eyes, two well formed nostrils, a full head of hair, and feet somewhat out of proportion to the body.

What he'd also drawn was two arms, with the right hand composed, quite correctly, of five fingers. But the left hand was resplendently adorned with six.

Six fingers?

It just so happens that I was born with six fingers. On my left hand.

I don't know whether this was just some coincidence, but I prefer to think of it as some kind of DNA memory - something that stirred in his sub-conscious – so he drew the extra digit as a symbol of our connection.

Am I reading something into it that you believe isn't there?

You're welcome to your opinion. But I prefer to treasure this drawing as something that will forever keep Simon and me connected.

10

Watch Out! Gravity Will Get You

When I was seven, life was fun. There was no pressure at school, no pressure at home, just endless opportunities to enjoy life.

And learn. Let's face it, seven-year-olds are sponges, looking at most things with new eyes and a hunger for information. They are questioners, never satisfied with a simple answer.

Every subject gets the full treatment – what, but why, but how? Parents and teachers bear the brunt of these inquisitions, but seven-year-olds don't restrict their questions only to these people.

Other seven-year-olds can be a source of knowledge, especially when no adults are around. Sadly this is often where education can take a detour into dodgy terrain.

Here's a classic example: my friend Robert Croly lived on the side of a steep hill. Clive Huskisson and I loved spending time playing in Robert's back yard.

The reason was simple – it ended at a cliff edge that plummeted about a hundred metres to a valley floor with a river flowing past a little way away.

Bent Thumb Thinking

But wait – there's more! The cliff had a cave.

This was a young boy's idea of heaven, because we could spend endless hours pretending to be explorers, pirates looking for treasure, cowboys chasing crooks, and more.

But there was one scary moment I'll never forget. A moment of learning.

Four or five of us had been tearing around, chasing imaginary bad guys, who'd given us the slip. We stood at the cliff edge, looking down over the valley below, and discussing what to do next.

"I need a pee," said one of the boys. That sounded like a great idea to all of us. Let's face it – young boys find it hard to resist an opportunity to pee from a great height.

All of us made ready to do this, except the first boy, who yelled: "WAIT!"

We froze in mid stream. What was wrong?

"Don't you know about gravity?"

This question shed no light on the anxiety we all suddenly felt. We shrugged our shoulders in unison.

"Gravity will get you!" Our paranoid friend stood there, looking over the cliff, and shaking his head.

"Whaddayamean?"

"You should never pee down a long drop, 'cos as it goes down, gravity gets it and it can pull your guts out!"

Imagine the picture – five boys, on the edge of a cliff, taps off, and scared silly.

We never questioned our friend, or his sources, but I never again saw one of that group of boys take a chance with gravity and its pulling power.

That was my first experience of science being used out of context to prove a mere theory. It still goes on today.

All I can say is, be careful who you listen to.

 "Ah, I can see it all. Another smile! Thanks, Graham"
– Kristin (Hungary)

11

Dad's Pontiac Takes A Hit

My dad loved big American cars. He had Buicks, Chevrolets, Oldsmobiles and Pontiacs. Most were left-hand-drives, in a country with right-hand-drive cars.

So as I grew up I became very proficient at being the right-hand set of eyes, which was an important role when dad wanted to overtake. From the left he couldn't always see clearly enough to judge whether he could pull out into the next lane.

On a holiday in Cape Town, our family was spread out in a huge blue and white Pontiac, cruising down the main street of a south-eastern suburb. I was in my preferred position – right behind the driver, with my mouth only inches from dad's right ear.

This was perfect for a boy who never stopped asking questions: is that car faster than ours, can that car do a hundred miles an hour, are British cars better than American cars, what size engine does that one have, and on and on. Why? How? When? If?

To his credit my dad answered most of my queries, and as we wallowed along that morning on soft springs propelled by effortless V8 power, I asked another question. And waited, knowing it often took a moment before the reply arrived.

But I waited, and waited. Then I noticed dad's shoulders shake slightly and rise sharply, his face contort wildly, and he let loose the most gigantic sneeze ever.

It took us all by surprise, including dad. In fact, especially dad, because, in the explosion of breath, he'd blown his false teeth right out of his mouth. The evidence was there for all four of us to see – a full set of dentures biting fiercely onto the steering wheel as if to secure their ride home.

Silence suddenly broke into wild, hysterical laughter and dad had to pull over and stop, so as not to cause an accident.

Once his teeth had been prized off the wheel and reinserted in his mouth we were able to proceed. The steering wheel bore no scars, but it changed my dad's sneezing process forever. Always after that a hand went up to catch what might come out, even when he was driving.

Cape Town, South Africa
December, 1956

 "That was so funny; I can almost hear the hysterical laughter in the car. Great story! Keep them coming as I always look forward to the next story."
—Therese

12

How Do You Measure a Mother's Love?

This is a story that took all of forty years to unfold. It is a tale of childhood anguish and adult understanding. Most of all, it is an illustration of how our incorrect perceptions can distort our relationships – even the closest ones.

Looking Through a Child's Eyes

You may, like me, have noticed how small children, hurt or upset, will seek out their mum for comfort and consoling in preference to Dad. Not always, but more often than not.

When you think about why, the answer is easy. In every case there was a nine month attachment between mother and child that no father can compete with.

Although that bond is not something we think about, I suppose we all feel it deep down, especially when we're young and vulnerable.

Even as a teenager, with that emotional myopia most teens suffer from, I didn't realise the dependence I had on my mum.

She'd always been there, always busy dedicating herself to the family, to what everyone else needed – which included me. It was never about what she needed.

Dad – well, he had other important things to do, like going to work and clubs and endless meeting. His priorities seemed to be elsewhere.

Like most children, without realising or appreciating it, I relied on my mother for so much. This meant that when I left home at the age of thirteen to go to boarding school, I felt very lost and alone. No family, along with the security that family life provides, remained.

But I missed mum the most. The umbilical cord of expectation was cut. Mum was far away and I was on my own, lonely, even though I was surrounded day and night by a horde of other boys.

Blessed (or cursed) with a lively imagination, I began to wonder if she missed me the way I missed her.

It only took a few months – second term – before a seed of doubt was sown. A nagging feeling about the extent of this maternal love began to grow. It was entirely illogical, but I was only thirteen.

What started it was simple and innocuous. Every week day, straight after lunch, the mail was distributed. Names were called out by the head prefect, and the boy whose name it was, went and collected his mail.

While other boys received their weekly letter from home, I waited for my name to be called out. It never did. The fact that most of the boys didn't see their parents at all during the twelve week terms, while I often did, was no consolation to my young heart.

I felt left out. And in my mind it was Mum's responsibility.

Mothers everywhere will feel the unfairness of this, but isn't it true that we have expectations of our mum that, for some reason, don't extend to our dad.

Never once did I wonder why my father didn't write. Subconsciously I never saw it as part of his job description. It fell into the category of what a mother does.

The lunchtime ritual continued and soon enough I stopped paying attention when names were called out. I never really dwelled on why my mum never wrote.

After five years of boarding school – years that gave me so much – it was my decision to spread my wings and live in places other than the home of my childhood. My first real job, for example, took me a thousand kilometres from my home town. Even my wedding was elsewhere.

Constantly changing cities, even countries, was part of the process of growing up and growing my own family when children arrived.

It was about this time that the dormant seed of doubt stirred from its slumber and began to bear it's bitter fruit again.

Throughout all the years of getting married, becoming a parent and living overseas, there were no letters, no birthday cards, no gifts. Not even for my children. It was boarding school all over again, but no longer confined to just me.

It hurt. It also humiliated me, because the apparent neglect placed my parents in a poor light, and I, in turn, felt this poor light reflected on me personally.

What do you do?

I knew what I wasn't going to do! I was definitely not going to write to them! Not a chance! Why would I, because there was not a chance they would write back?

That was how I felt about this "maternal" negligence. It was my mother who'd made the choice, so she was going to face the consequences, and by default, so was my dad.

The thinking was simple: if you don't write to me, I won't write to you! Translated that meant:

If you don't love me, I won't love you!

A Child's Thoughts Mould an Adult's Life

Three decades of not writing went by.

Oh, there was communication, but it was almost always initiated from my side, and usually by phone. To her great credit my wife, Gaynor, sent birthday cards, Christmas cards and gifts, throughout all those years.

But she wasn't the one who'd suffered! It was me who'd been deprived initially and then humiliated.

These, of course, were not my conscious thoughts, but now that I reflect, they must have been close to what drove me to refuse writing to parents growing older and living on another continent, far away.

Our relationship was perfectly amicable – even loving. But why no birthday cards, at least for my children, to show that their grandparents loved and valued them? And was there anything I could do about it?

The answer was waiting for me in a book.

Author, Stephen Covey, confronted me with a question. What he posed was to do with the difference between being reactive or proactive. The first, he explains in his book, is allowing the actions of another person to determine how we respond to them. The other is acting independently of how another person treats us.

My first thought was that 'proactive' described me pretty much correctly. I felt confident that no-one controlled my actions but me.

But then I started thinking…

For weeks, off and on, I ran past incidents through my mind, analysing how I'd responded to them.

It must have been at least a month of mulling before I thought about letters and mum. Was my decision not to write to my mother reactive or proactive?

Ouch!

It didn't take much consideration to know the answer. So I decided, proactively, that failure in the past didn't have to translate to a future of similar consequences. If I wanted to be in control of me, I should put my pride aside and start writing.

This is what I did.

Sunday afternoon from then on, at around five, I sat down at my computer and wrote a letter to Mum – and the rest of the family overseas. Then I printed it out and faxed it to my sister on the other side of the Indian Ocean. She would find it at her desk the next morning and deliver it to our parents on her way home that same day.

It was a good set up. All I had to do was write.

The letter itself needed to be general news, about my family, what was going on locally, and totally unconditional. Questions were out, because asking assumed an answer – a return letter – and that was not the purpose of me writing.

As the weeks and months and years went by, the letter count rose. Truthfully, I did have occasional hopes that my actions would precipitate a response – a card or letter coming back.

Nothing!

Two and a half years of this one-way letter writing went by. That's a lot of Sundays, and a ream of letters filled with cheery chatter and children's achievements.

I often wondered what was going on at the receiving end. Were the letters received? Were they read? More importantly, were they appreciated? But I couldn't ask. Why? Because that would, in effect, be asking for something in return. And the rules I'd set myself stated that to do that was a breach.

And so the Sundays rolled on.

Then I received a phone call. It stopped the process temporarily and led me back to my mother's side.

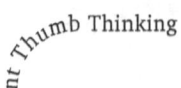
Bent Thumb Thinking

Growing Up Means Putting Away Childish Nonsense

My mother had been diagnosed with advanced lung cancer. My sister advised that I should get there urgently.

It took a little over twenty-four hours and I was there. The news was told to me by Dad and sister separately, each with their own perspective of what the medical people had said, and each with their own version of how the events would play out in the weeks and months ahead.

Mum herself was apologetic about the fuss she was causing. She smiled, sitting in her chair, wrapped in a blanket that made her seem even tinier and more fragile than she really was. Her voice was so quiet I had to strain to hear.

All day we spoke, of old times – happy times. Holidays in country cabins, and shows we'd been to as a family. Always in the past.

On the day before I was due to depart for home, with my mind full of the memories of my youth, I dared to wonder.

"Why, in ten days of chatting about the things important to Mum has she said nothing about my letters?"

Would I ask? Should I ask? Was asking going to break that rule?

I decided.

"Mum, you know I've been writing letters to you and Dad every Sunday for a while. You do receive them, don't you?"

She turned and looked up at me sitting beside her, and smiled weakly.

"Oh yes. I've kept all of them."

Then she stood up slowly and shuffled to her bedroom. A minute went by and she returned with something in her hand.

She sat down and started turning the pages of a pile of documents, bulldog clipped, and as thick as two fingers.

"I've kept every one of them. Every week I read all of them. Even the old ones."

Again she turned and looked at me and smiled.

"When I read them it makes me feel as though I'm with you and Gaynor and those precious children. That's why I read them over and over. Even the old ones."

In a matter of moments that childhood seed of doubt had been revealed as quite unfounded. To this day I still don't know why she never wrote, but I do know it was not because she didn't care.

I sat and smiled silently at my mum. There was nothing more to say.

 "Glad I heard about you and your stories. Thanks for allowing us into your world. This one really touched my heart. The word 'mum' is such a beautiful one and every 'mum' special in her own right."

– Deb Stevens

13

Four Mothers In my Life

We only ever have one mother, physiologically. That's a fact. But there are other significant people in our life we unconsciously consider as mothers too.

I can count four.

The first, of course, was my actual mum – she, who gave birth to me and took care of me through my childhood.

Joan, her name was. She was dedicated to her children, my sister and me, almost to the point of excluding most other aspects of her life. She was devoted to us and provided a model to me of what a woman should be – gentle, kind, concerned and caring. Food in particular was her love language. Every problem could be fixed with food, was how my mother Joan always operated.

That's what I saw in my mother, and she was the most important female in my young life. Oh, she was also quiet.

So it's interesting to reflect on just how much those qualities influenced my perceptions.

Then, when I was twenty, I met Mrs. Smith. We hit it off immediately. For the first time I recognised the inner strength so many women have. She was interesting and interested. We spoke about my university studies, my opinions about current affairs. And then she told me her opinion.

These weren't deep intellectual conversations, but they opened up a realm that was new to me. Mrs. Smith was solid – steady. If we disagreed she was quite happy to continue talking without reacting. So in a way she was also quiet.

There grew an instant closeness between us, which was wonderful.

Wonderful it was for more than one reason. Mrs. Smith was, you see, the mother of a certain Miss Smith – first name Gaynor – and Gaynor had captured a very significant amount of my attention. This began the first time I saw her.

The good news is that, having become close with Mrs. Smith, I proceeded painfully slowly to become even closer with her daughter. And so, when Gaynor and I married, Mrs. Smith became mum to me, and we lived happily ever after. I loved her, and I think she loved me.

But that is not the end of the story.

Within a few short years there were two babies who's mother I was married to. A pigeon pair they used to call them – a boy and a girl – with Gaynor playing mum to both them and, if I'm honest, me as well.

She'd learned a certain range of skills from her mother, and we were the beneficiaries. To her credit, Gaynor has always acknowledged the powerful role her mother played in forming her values and beliefs. Oh, she is also quiet, but never cowering.

Gaynor looked after us. She cared for us so well that we flourished. Home was always a haven for the three of us, and our friends loved the warm and inviting places where we lived. I'm talking about the friends of our children as well as our adult friends.

That's always testimony to a woman's touch. Every single man's home I've ever been in has, somehow, and in my opinion only, been the poorer for not having a woman's touch to transform it.

And so to the final mum in my life.

As our two pigeons grew up and flew the coop, one of them became a mother in her own right. I'm pleased to say the egg never drops far from the mother bird.

Our daughter, with obvious help from Cameron, gave birth to a boy who is one of the greatest joys of my life. Being the mother of my grandson makes her even more of a significant mum in my life.

As we've watched the baby grow into a boy, soon to be a young man, we've watched his mother grow in confidence and competence as a mum.

And quietly, observing from a somewhat objective view, I can see the very distinctive maternal wisdom I first noticed in my mother-in-love, flowing strongly through the lives of the two mothers who followed her. Is she quiet? You'll get different answers depending on who you ask.

How good it is occasionally to stop and reflect on mums in general and our own mum in particular.

Of course they would not be mothers without there being a father somewhere in the picture, so this discourse does not ignore the part that dads all play. It is simply a moment where I've zoomed in on the bigger picture, to identify just why we love our mums.

I love my mums – all four of them.

14

Help!

I spent a day at a hospital recently.

During that time I had consultations with my neurologist, an occupational therapist, a speech pathologist, a dietitian and a dentist.

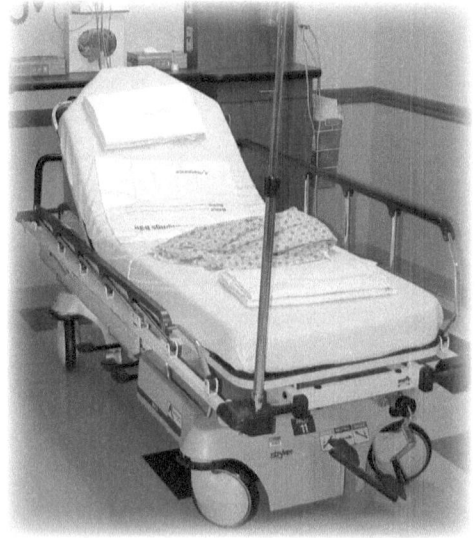

Each one of them was focussed entirely on helping me – on making my life easier, safer and possibly even more productive.

I left there exhausted. Grateful, but drained. This got me thinking about how I have always viewed people helping me. My suspicion is that the way I still feel about it is quite common, especially among males.

For most men the decision to accept help is an admission of weakness – "I have a problem." And actually asking for help is a giant step further than merely accepting it when it's offered.

This behaviour starts when we're young – not even out of nappies.

Picture the one-year-old. Taking those first uncertain steps. One, two, maybe three, then crash. Parents ecstatic, enthusiastic, proud.

"Good boy! Good girl! Come on. Again! Uppies!"

In a matter of days that same child, who couldn't take one step without a helping hand, is now venturing off with giggles and dancing eyes, navigating their way from one piece of supporting furniture to another, unafraid of falling, desperate to expand the boundaries of their upright adventures.

As adults and parents we hold our breath and stretch out our hands, eager to encourage, but focussed more specifically on catching them when they fall. We're there to help.

And within those few short days most toddlers are so intent on their newfound independence that they move in any direction except where the outstretched arms are waiting.

If they could speak at that stage, I'm sure the majority of children would be saying something like this:

"No, no! I don't want you to help me. I want to do it myself. This is how I learn. Get out of my way!"

Fortunately for our feelings, toddlers can't talk, so we persevere with our offers of assistance. And in the broader scheme of things that's a good thing.

Children need to grow up feeling they have people they can fall back on for help. Or at least, lean on in times of need.

But why is it we want so badly to be independent – to refuse the help, deny any need? Especially males.

The African proverb about it taking a whole village to raise a child is a truth. Yet in life this issue of help seems always to be viewed through a pair of binoculars.

On the one hand we look at family members, friends and others around us with the binoculars held the right way around. This brings them closer, so we can observe them and better understand how we can help if it's needed. We want to know more – to relate better. In this way we can more easily live by the good old Golden Rule, treating them with kindness and care. Loving our neighbours.

But on the other hand, when it comes to our own personal needs, we so often have the binoculars turned backwards – pushing reality further away, making it smaller, more distant. Less important. We see our own needs diminished, less worthy of consideration.

So our answer, quite regularly, when we're offered assistance is: "No, no. Really! I'm OK. I don't need help."

Even if nobody notices when we're struggling, the last thing we consider doing is to put up our hand and say: "Help".

Is that everyone, or just me?

Do we become permanently locked into that inner child's fight for freedom? Is independence eternally so attractive that we become entrenched in the habit of finding it at the expense of accepting a helping hand occasionally?

If this is the case, there's a definite disconnect in our ability to develop relationships. After all, relationships are based on trust between two people, and if you trust someone, do you refuse to disclose your struggles? Do you refuse to accept their assistance? Do you shut the door on your vulnerability?

Men, mostly, have that door locked – barricaded. Permanently.

But there's a big price we pay for this privacy. I would suggest that any close, strong, lasting relationship needs the binoculars working the right way regarding others and ourselves.

Let me tell you a little story about how "help" helped me.

We were happily married, with an eighteen month old boy and a baby on the way.

Having just returned to Johannesburg after living in Montreal for a year, I was back with the company that had given me my first job. The pay was reasonable, but we'd sold everything to travel overseas. So we had nothing.

Weekends were austere. Living in a converted stable on a small farm meant lots of fresh air and space to spread out, but we were struggling.

Quite regularly on a Wednesday or Thursday, my phone would ring at work. (We didn't have a home phone and mobiles were decades away.)

"Hello, Graham speaking…"

"Hi Graham, it's Ken."

Ken was Ken Funston, an ex-Springbok cricketer who'd toured Australia in the fifties. He'd also played soccer with my dad in Pretoria years earlier and Ken and his wife had become close friends of my parents.

Now they were our friends, filling two roles in our young adult lives – surrogate parents, which was wonderful considering our real parents were a long way away, and big brother and sister, offering support and encouragement in a way parents find hard to do.

"Are you doing anything special this weekend?" asked Ken.

"No, we're not," I answered with absolute certainty, because we almost never did anything special at that particular stage of our lives.

"Oh good! I need a bit of help with something, and you're the person for the job."

"What job?"

"Don't worry about that now. How about you three come over on Sunday, say about ten? Then I can show you what I need help with."

"Sounds great," I responded.

"And stay for lunch, of course," added the very generous Ken.

He didn't have any idea how pleased I was to be able to help, whatever it was he needed done. And he didn't know how much we enjoyed the company and the marvellous sense of support they gave us. Not to mention the food.

We were new-ish at being married, even newer at being parents, and I was in a relatively new job, living in an unfamiliar city a long way from our families. So it was a somewhat daunting world, and we had little life experience to base our decisions on. A day spent with the Funstons was priceless.

With them there was mentoring of a kind that was so gentle we didn't realise it was happening. Ken and I discussed my career, my role as a young father, and my past sporting feats, even though he was the real sports star. Being the best kind of big brother, he shone the spotlight on me.

Gaynor and Marie spoke about marriage, motherhood and many more topics women consider important. There was wisdom imparted that Gaynor still refers to today.

"Ken phoned me today. He wants me to help him with something on Sunday," I explained when I got home that day.

"What's he want help with?" Gaynor asked.

"Don't know, but he's invited us to stay for lunch," I explained.

"Oh, goody," enthused Gaynor, always happy for a chance to hang out with Marie.

When Sunday arrived we were off and running, relishing the thought of being with this couple and their four children.

Morning tea with scones and jam was ready when we arrived, and after all the fussing over a very engaging toddler, otherwise known as our son, Ken and I went outside.

"Graham, I need some very good coals for a braai (South African for 'barbeque'), and I'm not very good at getting the fire just right."

"Oh, OK," I muttered, surprised it was such a simple job.

"I know how good you are. You've been doing it since you were a little chap, haven't you?"

Ken smiled and I beamed. In those days every young South African male prided himself on his braai-ing prowess, and I was no different. This was high praise from someone I admired.

"We've invited some friends over for lunch, so we need coals that won't burn the meat, but won't go out too quickly."

"Leave it to me," I replied, my young male ego celebrating this trust with such an important task. "I can also do the cooking."

Ken nodded and put an arm around my shoulder, which said how grateful he was that he could depend on me.

It all sounds so silly and puerile now, but we forget how big such small gestures can be in the process of our development. I glowed in this relationship with a sporting legend who was almost twenty years older than me, but who made me feel so valued and respected. He needed my input. I loved that.

At the end of the day, driving home with an exhausted child asleep in the back of the car, Gaynor asked me a question.

"So what was it Ken wanted you to help him with?"

"Oh, the fire for the braai," I answered.

"Really? But he can make a fire himself, can't he? I think it must have been something else," she continued.

"Maybe, but if it was, he didn't get round to it. Nice day though."

"It's always nice being with them."

I nodded in agreement. It was a happy day whenever we spent it with the Funstons. Looking back, they made us feel more grown up than we actually were, and that's a good feeling. And Ken's secret strategy for making me feel this way was simply to ask for help.

Decades later that request for help had an unexpected consequence. By now we were living in Melbourne, Australia. My phone rang. It was Ken, asking if he and Marie could spend a few days with us on their way from New Zealand back to their home in South Africa.

The reply was instant.

"Yes! Of course!"

We were thrilled by the prospect of seeing these people who'd been so supportive in our younger days. And we hadn't spent time with them in years.

It was two weeks before they were due to arrive, so we planned a number of activities to make their stay enjoyable.

One of these was a visit to the famous MCG – the Melbourne Cricket Ground – where we knew Ken had played against the Australians in the summer of 1952-53.

By a stroke of luck we had a friend who worked for Cricket Australia. He was duly contacted about the possibility of arranging a special tour of the great stadium.

"I can do better than that," Ray responded enthusiastically. "Leave it to me."

On the appointed day we arrived at the MCG and were welcomed by our friend. He then escorted us into the cricket museum, into the old scoreboard and eventually out onto the hallowed turf.

As we stood there, in the middle of this historic arena, I noticed Marie take Ken's hand and gently wind her arm into his – supportively. Ken's face bore a smile, but there were tears rolling down his cheeks, moved by the memories.

Slowly we ambled off, climbing the stairs and following our very gracious host.

"You will join us for lunch, won't you," queried Ray.

We all nodded as we were welcomed into the dining room, a place filled with various precious fragments of the past, including table service so respectful it seemed we'd moved very appropriately and seamlessly back into the nineteen fifties.

Ken had recovered from his moment of emotion by now, but was confronted by a new challenge to his feelings.

There to welcome him stood three past Australian cricketers, one of whom – Colin McDonald – had been captain of the side Ken played against in that tour.

Hands were warmly shaken, seats were taken slowly, and then our host said he had a small presentation to make.

Ken, who never liked making a fuss, sat open mouthed as Ray said a few kind words and handed over a folder. Inside it was a copy of the scorecard for the second Test Match that Ken had played in on the MCG.

Choking back the tears, my wonderful "older brother" spoke with such humility about how grateful he was for the effort these people had made to be there and how he would treasure this occasion in the same way he treasured his cricketing memories from this famous venue.

It was an emotional time for me as well. I was witnessing a hero of my heart being gracious, generous in his gratefulness, and always humble, even though he had so much he could have boasted about.

He was quietly mentoring me again.

And, in a strange way, this guidance hinged on a simple, innocuous question:

"Graham, can you help me?"

Asking for help is not always a sign of weakness. Quite often it's an invitation to come a little closer and engage yourself in that person's life. And you, not they, are the major beneficiary.

In a similar way, when you are in need of help, but refuse to ask for it, you're denying someone, as well as yourself, the opportunity of coming closer and possibly, just possibly, enhancing the relationship between the two of you.

And what is life without relationships? I suggest the answer is "a lonely place".

15

Granny Finds Out From A Four-Year-Old

The most honest people in the world are…four-year-olds.

There's no sugar coating. No politeness. Just the unadulterated truth, especially with regard to what they think. They are naïve enough to tell you what they really think.

Never has this been more clearly demonstrated to me than when our daughter Ande – the sweetest, quietest, gentlest child – was with us spending time with Gaynor's parents.

Appropriately, Simon was deeply attached to his grandfather, George, and enjoyed going to work with him at the Kimberley museum.

Ande, on the other hand, loved her Granny Clara. She was a shadow, in the kitchen, around the house and even shopping.

This adoration created a wonderful bond between two people precious to me. It was something I could never form in the same way with my daughter. So I observed, nodding my head silently in approval. This was good – for Ande, for Granny Clara and for Gaynor and me. If Ande, as she grew up, could emulate in some way the characteristics of her grandmother, she'd do very well indeed. Good role model, is what I thought.

But the relationship hit a snag one hot summer evening.

For a week the shadow had followed grandma around everywhere. Well, almost everywhere. There were, naturally, certain places that required some privacy. One of them was the bathroom.

In the house there was no shower – only a bath. And Granny Clara, with guests in the house, putting herself last in line for the bath, often found the best time was late afternoon.

This time coincided with Ande becoming a little bored, so she'd been pestering to have her bath at the same time.

"Can I bath with you, Granny Clara?" begged this little poppet of a child.

"Oh, Ande, let your gran have some time on her own," instructed Gaynor.

And that's how it went for days on end. Remember, four-year-olds are some of the most persistent people on the planet. "No", simply means "Not this time, but keep trying".

Eventually the fateful day arrived.

"Granny Clara, can I bath with you?" asked Ande.

"But we're going for a walk in the park," Gaynor reminded.

"She can stay with me," stated Granny Clara. "We can have a cup of tea, and then have a bath."

Ande's eyes, which were large anyway, widened in surprise. Her perseverance had paid off. This was excitement indeed.

Shaking her head, Gaynor turned and, like a mother duck, led Simon and me down the garden path, out the gate and off to the park.

Kimberley, for all that it is on the edge of the Kalahari Desert, had a beautiful botanic garden, originally planted in the halcyon days of the diamond rush.

We wandered around, read the various tree tags, and generally enjoyed ourselves. Around an hour later we arrived back at the house, to find Granny Clara and Ande sitting on the front verandah sipping cool drinks. They were both gleaming fresh, soaped and scrubbed and wearing clean clothes. Towels were wrapped around their still wet hair.

"Hi," we said.

"Hello," said the washed ladies. "How was your walk? The park's so pretty and peaceful, isn't it?" commented grandma.

We nodded in agreement.

"How was your bath?" Gaynor asked, concerned that her mum had not been too put out by her granddaughter.

Granny Clara, her arm around Ande, nodded her head and said: "We had fun, didn't we?"

She looked down to check that Ande agreed. She stared into her glass of orange cordial and said nothing.

"Was it fun?" asked Gaynor.

Ande nodded, but said nothing.

"Well, you wanted to bath with Gran," prodded Gaynor.

Again Ande nodded, still peering into her glass. Then she spoke.

"Granny Clara…"

"Yes," replied grandma.

"Granny Clara, you look much better with clothes on!"

There was a sudden silence. We wondered how Granny Clara would take this adjudication.

We looked at Ande and then at Gaynor's mum. She, in turn, looked from us to Ande, hugged her even tighter and kissed her on the forehead.

"Out of the mouth of babes…" she said, with a wide grin on her face.

That broke the ice and we laughed. In fact, much of Kimberley laughed, because wherever she went Granny Clara told the story.

Perhaps one of the benefits of growing up as the eldest of eight children, in a tiny rural town, is that you learn never to take yourself too seriously, and that the funniest jokes are when it's a laugh at your own expense.

Granny Clara, my mother-in-love, was very much like that.

16

Men May Be Brave But Woman Are Tough

The title of this story is, I concede, controversial. It's also a sweeping statement, with a myriad of exceptions, I'm sure. But on the occasion about which this tale is based, the statement was true on both counts. As a matter of fact, it may be more correct to have said: 'Men may be too brave and women too tough for their own good'. Are Gaynor and I unusual in this way? I don't think so.

We were young, my wife and I. We were also fit and, you might say, a little bit foolish.

Our children were away visiting grandparents during the school holidays, so we decided to do something we'd wanted to do for years – walk in the Cedarberg Mountains two hours drive north of Cape Town.

We were not mountaineers or climbers, just people who enjoyed the open air and each other's company. So the way we prepared was simple.

We found out that there was a three-day walk around a particular peak – I think called Krakadouw – on a farm. Apparently the farmer was friendly and allowed a small number of people to do the walk at any given time. I called up and we were on the list that included only one other group at that time.

The equipment, by today's standards, was rudimentary: a tiny tent, a portable stove, powdered food, a warm coat, boots and basic clothing. It was early autumn, which sounded like sunny days and cool nights.

On the allotted day we set off from home and drove to the farm. The farmer was, indeed, friendly. He explained that we could park our car and pick it up when we returned. It was also required that we write the details of our planned progress in a register, just in case.

It was about eleven by the time we set off, intending to walk until we reached a spot the farmer had advised was good for spending the night. In our minds it would be a joy to be out under the stars, our cares left far behind. We could relax and let the worries of the daily grind wash away.

We walked. We talked. We pointed at views across the valley. We wowed and whistled at the scenery as it unfolded.

The first hour was along a well-used farm track, which made the going easy. But then, through a gate and instructed by a faded wooden signpost, we struck off along a path through low scrub. The farmer had given us a hand-drawn map that showed that there were cairns all along the way to guide us. He hadn't told us that these were often a kilometre apart and hard to see if you were new at the game.

We stopped for lunch – sandwiches and tea – surrounded by mountains and valleys glowing in the afternoon light.

Then we walked again. Hours went by, and the cloudless sky went wispy, then grey. In no time we were walking into a bleak and threatening wind. Over a mountain stream we skipped, deciding that if the weather turned we'd stop early, pitch our tent and wait for the morning. It would almost certainly be better then.

Five hours into our walk we could not find the next cairn, with the gloom and now a soft drizzle cutting our visibility. The smart thing to do was to find a piece of level ground on the mountainside, and set up camp.

So we did. The tiny tent went up in a few minutes, and we crawled inside to make tea. It was around four o'clock, which was too early for our evening meal, but definitely time for something hot, because in the last hour we'd become wet and cold.

In the confines of the tent the little cooker began to heat the water and the atmosphere. It was reminiscent of those wonderful times as a child spent making cosy spaces by draping blankets and sheets over chairs, then sitting inside eating cookies, cut off from the outside world. A primeval sort of safety, secure inside our cave.

But the wind cranked up a notch or three. Our tent began to sag a bit. Brave me, the man, said I'd venture out to tighten the ropes, while Gaynor prepared the tea.

I was out there for longer than either of us expected. We conversed, because only a paper thin sheet of fabric separated us, but the wind was wailing through the scrub and shaking the walls of the tent, so our voices were challenged to overcome the storm.

By the time I'd completed my task I was mildly concerned with our predicament. But when I unzipped the tent flap and stuck my head in the conversation turned from matter-of-fact observations, to all out debate.

"Have a look out here," I suggested. "It's sleeting."

My wife peered out and, in a voice that didn't need volume for me to realise the gravity of her concern, said: "That's not sleet! That's a snow storm!"

I climbed into the tent, zipped up the door, and the two of us looked at each other. This had never been in the plans. This called for serious thinking. The decisions we made in the next few minutes would be critical to our safety.

What should we do?

We disagreed entirely. Our ideas were diametrically different.

All my experience in the mountains and on bush walks had taught me that walking when visibility is poor, and particularly at night, is close to suicidal. So my inclination was to hunker down and wait for better weather. We'd taken five hours to get this far, so going back would mean it would be hours after sunset before we arrived at the farm.

Gaynor looked at other details. Our tent was struggling to stay up. Our clothes were wet – even the extras, because our rucksacks had leaked. And a snow storm might trap us here for days, so our food supplies would run out.

"I want to go back," she said, with a determination accentuated by her starting to pack up.

"We can't. It'll be dark in an hour and a half, and we could hardly find the cairns when the sun was out. It's too dangerous."

"I want to go. If we don't, and we get stuck here, that'll be even worse."

Everything I knew about survival said "No!" but either way, we were in an awkward situation. Whichever choice we made, there were serious dangers and opportunities for disaster.

"We can get back much faster than we got here," Gaynor pleaded.

My choice was made. We'd go.

"OK, but you need to go in front and set the pace. I'll be able to keep up," I instructed.

"No, no. You go in front and I'll hang onto your rucksack."

By now we'd jammed all the wet equipment and the waterlogged tent into their receptacles, slung them on our backs and had started the long haul home to the farmhouse. It was around five o'clock.

We walked. We scrambled. We went the way that seemed right, without seeing the cairns, or consulting the map. Snow turned to sleet and then to driving rain, so there was no time to lose. I strode out at a speedy clip, and Gaynor, for most of the way, trotted behind me, talking quietly to stay in touch.

Over rocks, across streams that were now flowing much higher than before, around bushes, sliding down embankments and then clambering up the other side, and on into the eastern gloom we tore.

Dusk turned to darkness at the end of the second hour, and on we plunged. The light faded, but we didn't. It was all a blur, with our instincts overriding our emotions and any logical thought about our plight.

We never stopped for a second, because every second was vital to our survival. I say that because walking in total darkness along the side of a mountain, weighed down by soaking wet rucksacks, out in the middle of nowhere, is incredibly dangerous.

And suddenly a gate appeared out of the darkness. It was the gate we'd gone through earlier, and meant we'd arrived back at the farm track. Pheew! From here we knew the way and it was guaranteed now that we'd get back safely.

It took us only thirty more minutes to the farmhouse, and when we arrived, only two and a half hours after making that monumental decision, I knocked on the door.

This stranger, who had only met us a few hours earlier and spent all of twenty minutes with us, opened the door with a flourish.

"Oh, man," he said in that unmistakeable South African style. "Am I glad to see you two! Man, I was so worried."

He took us inside and explained that whenever the weather turned the way it had, walkers could get trapped for weeks, and even rescue helicopters were unable to fly into the area because of the wind force around the mountain peaks.

Then he showed us into a little, ramshackled cottage

nearby, lit the fire and brought us steaming bowls of lamb and veggie soup and told us again how relieved he was that we'd got back.

With a huge wood fire blazing, we hung our equipment out to dry and then began undressing. Boots always come off first, but Gaynor couldn't get her left one to budge. I helped by giving it a tug.

The result was a scream of pain.

We realised that the reason the boot could not be removed was a massively swollen ankle. Gaynor, in the process of keeping up with the pace I'd set coming back, had turned it and sprained it.

A knife was needed to finally remove the boot, and by the morning the swelling had reached proportions that indicated the severity of the injury. It was bad! But in the all out rush for safety, not a step had been missed. Gaynor tried to remember when it might have happened, and could only speculate that it was done when she slid down a riverbed onto a rocky area.

I carried Gaynor to the car the next morning, having thanked the farmer for his hospitality and the painkillers he provided. She slept all the way home, having been in agony all through the night, as I snored happily beside her.

In the car were two people – the brave man prepared to stay and fight against the storm, and the woman who was tough and smart enough to make the decision to cut and run when staying was a danger too great.

We survived that adventure and lived to do many other exciting and slightly foolish things – together.

 "Damn good story, Graham. Was on the edge of my seat, shallow breathing. Knew you would get out but the how was amazing."
– **Yvonne Johnson**

17

Ring, Ask, Marry – A Three-Part Adventure of the Heart

This may sound trite and self-serving to some, but the truth is I feel I've lived a blessed life. And the biggest blessing was finding a life partner. The steps it took provided some funny stories attached to it.

The processes that turned my girlfriend into my fiancée and then my wife were not, I suspect, in keeping with normal procedures. My life has never been that straightforward. Here's an example – the first act in this three-part drama.

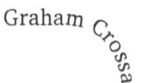

Part 1: Diamonds Are A Man's Biggest Challenge

We were in love, Gaynor and I, although I'd been in love for some time longer than her, if you follow my meaning. It was my heart that had led the way in our relationship.

Then I moved away. All the way to Johannesburg I went, to find a job. Gainfully employed, I then travelled every weekend or so to be with Gaynor. Five hours each way was the short trip, to Kimberley; nine hours was the other, all the way to where Gaynor was still at university.

It was wearing me out, not to mention my diminutive one litre Austin Mini. The long all-night drives were also putting a strain on many Monday mornings at work, because on more than one occasion I drove straight to the office without going home.

So I decided to take the plunge and have us back together. Engagement was the step indicated by convention, and even though I did not hold closely to convention, this seemed the right move.

To ask someone to marry you, convention again stipulates a particular procedure involving a diamond ring. And once again, not holding closely to convention, yours truly chose to do something most people do – that is to go to a jewellery store.

It so happened that Gaynor lived in the then diamond capital of the world. Kimberley is where de Beers had grown into an international company controlling the majority of diamond sales around the globe.

During my visits I'd met several people who worked for the company, and with the most honourable intentions in mind, I approached one for advice on how to "cut out the middle man". After all, I was a young man with big dreams but a small bank balance, so this seemed like a good way to optimise my buying power.

A phone call to this person started with a request from me to keep the purchase confidential. I didn't want Gaynor to know my intentions before I saw her. I also explained what I wanted and the amount of money I was prepared to spend. It was several month's earnings for me at that time.

"Leave it with me for a day or two and I'll see what I can do," the person replied. I did. Two days later I received a call.

"I've organised a beautiful stone for you. If you go to our head office in Johannesburg at midday the day after tomorrow with the money, my associate, Peter, will meet you on the steps outside. He'll give you the diamond."

"Oh great! Thank you so much for all your help," I blustered, feeling relieved that he'd done me such an enormous favour. I'd been so sure buying a diamond was going to be far more difficult, but I'd never bought one before, so, in truth I had no real idea of the processes or the potential problems.

Two days later I made sure I was on the steps with the money in an envelope. Johannesburg back then was no place to be wandering around with large amounts of cash in your pocket, so I was a little apprehensive.

Now, the big problem was this – how would I recognise Peter? (That was not his name. I've long forgotten what his real name was.)

I stood there, staring around. It was lunchtime, so there was a crowd. Any number of people could have been the one I was supposed to meet, but I didn't know what or who to look for.

Time ticked by. My mind began to play games. Did I have the wrong day? Had something happened, like an unexpected meeting, and the guy had been delayed? Or had the diamond not arrived in Johannesburg, but he didn't know how to contact me? Was I on the right steps? Anything was possible.

"Are you Graham?"

It was a voice from a mouth very near to my right ear. I jumped.

"Uh, yu...yu...yes. Are you Peter?"

"Yah, that's me. You've come for the diamond?"

"Yes," I said, settling down from my scare and remembering why I was there.

"Have you got the money?"

"Oh…yes," I replied, quickly removing the thick envelope from my jacket pocket and handing it over. He held out his hand, took the envelope, squeezed it as if weighing it somehow to be sure it was the right amount. Then he pocketed it and pulled out a flimsy folded sliver of tissue paper.

"The diamond's in there. It's a beauty. Careful when you unfold the paper."

With that he turned, jumped two steps to the top of the stairway, and disappeared into the imposing office building.

I stood there for a long moment, holding the tissue paper parcel, thinking how matter-of-fact it had all been. Then I stuffed my purchase into my pocket, thought about how Gaynor would react to the proposal, and went striding back to work. Smiling. She was going to be so surprised!

Back at my desk I resisted the temptation to look at what my money had bought. Only when I arrived home that evening did I clear a space on my little table, switch the desk lamp on, and carefully unfold the paper.

What lay there gleaming in the light was the most beautiful – and expensive – item I'd ever bought. I was enthralled. This was to symbolise how I felt about…

Hang on! At twenty-three I was not really into mushy romantic reflection. I was in love, but that didn't mean I was openly mooshy. So I refolded the paper, made myself a mug of hot tea and wondered briefly how I'd present the diamond. Within not much more than a minute I was reading a car magazine – a much more comfortable endeavour – and thinking about the next Grand Prix at Kyalami raceway, just a short distance from where I sat.

Three long weeks later I climbed into my Mini and went screaming down the "no speed limit" highway to meet Gaynor…and propose. Not for a moment during the nine hour journey did I consider the details of the transaction that had taken place to acquire the gemstone. Maybe I should have, but I didn't. No receipt, no counting the money, no surnames or formal identification documents had been used. It was just a simple exchange.

Was I simple too? Was my naivety so severe that I'd given these aspects of normal transactions no thought at all? I didn't know. I'd never bought a diamond before. And this, in my mind, was like buying wholesale. It didn't exactly follow convention. Ah, well...

To this day I assume all was above board. I'd never intended to do anything shifty, and the person who'd arranged it...I never did see him ever again. He moved to another job, I believe, in another city.

FOOTNOTE

On the Saturday afternoon Gaynor and I went for a drive. With a beautiful view of the ocean filling the windscreen, I parked and took a deep breath.

"I've got a present for you," I mumbled, steadfastly staring at the sea.

"Oh, what?" asked a smiling and instantly excited Gaynor, looking around for something gift-wrapped.

"Here," I replied, digging into my shirt pocket. What came out was a now wrinkled and twisted tissue paper item. I held it out and Gaynor took it, a look of curiosity on her face.

"What is it?" she asked.

"Open it," Mr. Smooth replied.

The tissue paper was unfolded and the contents sparkled magnificently. It was a beautiful diamond.

"What's this?" asked Gaynor, who knew what a diamond looked like.

"You know," I muttered, staring out to sea. This wasn't going the way I'd planned or expected.

"I know it's a diamond...but what does it mean?"

I thought the answer was so obvious that it didn't need to be articulated.

"You know," I repeated.

"Sorry, but that's not good enough. You can't just..."

My heart sank. Did I really have to ask – use words that were embarrassing for a twenty-three-year-old male like me.

"If this is what I think it is all about, you're going to have to ask," Gaynor continued.

The upshot of this was a mumbling, ineloquent proposal from a wimp – me. The good news was that when I'd finished asking if she'd marry me, she smiled again.

"Of course I will. You just needed to ask."

The next day I rode off into the sunset. A happy man at the start of what has been a wonderful journey. I didn't know it as I drove back in time to be at my desk on Monday morning, but there were more funny situations waiting for me before we said: "I do".

 "Graham, loved the first part of the adventure. Can hardly wait for 'the ask'! You are so clever, 'Mr Smooth'."

– Bruce Duperouzal

18

Ring, Ask, Marry – Part Two

Asking for permission to marry Gaynor

In Part 1 you will have read that I'd bought the diamond, begged the question, of my reluctance to actually speak the words: "Will you marry me?" and that I would gladly have stopped at handing over the diamond. But Gaynor had been adamant. "You've got to say the words, Graham".

I did, but now I faced an even more daunting task.

I've always believed that actions speak louder than words, but found out, forcibly, that there are exceptions to every rule. And now I needed to front up and ask Mr. Smith for permission to marry his daughter.

Here's the second act in this three-part drama.

Mothers-In-Law Have A Reputation, But Fathers-In-Law Are Different?

After all the romance of presenting a gleaming, glinting diamond to Gaynor in the front seat of my Mini, I took it back. No, not the offer of marrying her – the rock. It needed to be set in a ring and I took on the task of finding a jeweller to do this.

Three weekends later, with the diamond still wrapped in its even scruffier tissue paper, I headed off for Kimberley, five hours away.

That time was taken up with my eyes on the road, but my mind on the coming conversation. I'd never done this before, so I had no idea what the protocol was when I fronted up to face Mr. Smith.

What I did know was that he was a quiet man. Self-contained. He had views, but generally kept them to himself. All my previous conversations with him had been brief, with me initiating the dialogue.

It wasn't that he was shy. Instead, I had the impression that this was a "man's man" – happy around male company, where speaking is not the prime reason for being together. Fishing, fixing a car or lighting a fire for a barbecue – those were more the reasons men got together.

Mrs. Smith was altogether different. She and I had hit it off from the moment we met. She loved a chat, loved to find out other people's views, and generally loved people. She brought a heartfelt warmth to my young life that was profound.

I've teased Gaynor often that her mum and I were an item long before Gaynor and I were. It was a mutual admiration that drew us together and never let go. Besides, she was the mother of the most "attractive" person I'd ever met.

As the miles sped by that Friday night I thought less about the conversation I was due to have, and more about the direction my life was taking. Married at twenty-three? Was that a good idea? Was I ready for this big step? Should we wait a year to have our wedding?

Before I'd figured out the answers to these critical questions I arrived at Number 2, Customs Street. Gaynor was outside on the front verandah, bright with excitement. She knew what I was there to do.

Inside, I was warmly greeted by the parents who were in the main bedroom, to the left of the front door. It was eleven o'clock and Mr. Smith was in bed, sipping on a Scotch and reading. He was in the first stages of cancer, so ran out of energy early every evening.

"How was the drive?" Mrs. Smith asked.

"Good thanks. There was a lot of traffic getting out of Jo'burg," I replied.

"What do you think of the new Ford Escort?" was Mr. Smith's contribution. His eyes never left a brochure he was paging through.

"Everyone says it's a good car," was my noncommittal answer.

"Crossflow cylinder head!" continued Mr. Smith. "Sounds good. Have you read anything about it?"

Gaynor, who'd sat on the foot of the bed, rolled her eyes briefly. Discussing cars was not what the visit was about, and her frustration was in direct proportion to her excitement about letting her parents know we were engaged.

"Umm! It's to do with getting the fuel mixture in…"

"And it develops 46 brake horsepower," he interrupted.

"Daddy…Graham's just got here. Give him a chance to…" Gaynor protested.

"Rack and pinion steering, too," enthused Mr. Smith, undaunted by this attempt to stop his enthusiasm for the most important subject of the day.

"Daddy!"

"GEORGE! I think Graham wants to ask you something." This was the strong voice of a good wife.

It was enough to do the trick. George – Mr. Smith – looked up from the Ford Escort brochure he'd been devouring for the past few hours and acknowledged that, yes, perhaps there was something else going on.

How Mrs. Smith had worked out that Gaynor and I had a special agenda that evening is testimony to the widespread belief that mothers know everything.

But now I had all eyes on me. Five hours of preparation went out the window. What was I planning to say? Couldn't remember.

"Um…well…Gaynor and I…No, I mean…um…Mr. Smith, I'd like to marry your…"

Before I could finish, Gaynor had jumped up and was imploring.

"Show them the diamond! Show them!"

Relieved to be doing something rather than speaking, I fished out the crumpled tissue paper and handed it to the person I hoped would be my father-in-law. He hadn't as yet answered my question, so it was still not a certainty.

He slowly unfolded the paper while Gaynor explained that her dad had worked in the diamond industry for a while. Then he inspected the contents. Carefully. Thoroughly.

"Nice stone. No flaws. Slight colour." He handed the diamond to his wife for her perusal.

I was happy he approved of the stone, but that was only symbolic of something I felt was far more precious.

He fingered the brochure, but looked straight at me.

"Will you look after my daughter?"

There was a depth to the question that struck me instantly. Here was a father confronted with the request to release his responsibility for looking after his daughter, and entrust that care to a young man he's got to know, but only superficially. And he was taking it very seriously.

With my heart pounding I opened my mouth and replied with all the earnestness I could muster. One word came out.

"Yes."

Gaynor and her mother hugged and dissolved into a tearful mess of joy. Mr. Smith, his fatherly duty completed for the night, sighed and sipped his whiskey.

"McPherson Strut front suspension…do you know anything about how that works?"

Footnote

Mr. Smith bought a brand new Ford Escort Mk. 1 some months later. It was an altogether good car and performed beautifully, lasting for many years. But the undertaking I made to him that night has lasted infinitely longer.

19

Ring, Ask, Marry – Part Three

Getting Married

I had the ring, I had my future father-in-law's blessing (I think), so the next step was obvious.

But there's the conventional wedding and there's the alternative. Guess which way ours went? That's right.

The conventional wedding, according to my observations, is bride-driven, over-organised, far too expensive and so stressful for the participants that it's more like a nightmare than a dream come true. It's just not enjoyable.

That's just my opinion. Ours was nothing like that.

Here's the final act in this three-part drama.

I'd Rather Have A Great Marriage Than A Great Wedding.

At the age of twenty-three I'd given absolutely no thought to marriage, or the idea of a wedding.

Yes, I know I'd bought a diamond, proposed, and even asked Mr. Smith for his consent. But I had definitely not extended my thinking to the actual wedding. Call me naïve, even negligent, but getting engaged in my mind didn't lead immediately to marriage. I was a guy, and somehow the dots hadn't connected completely in my young head.

The way I saw it, we could wait as long as we liked. Do it all in our own sweet time. We were in control. And life just then was wonderful, so why change it?

That sounds all well and good, but the decision to get married was made only a few short months later.

In our favour was youth. We had no set plans, but a great sense of adventure. Thinking back, we were amazingly confident in the way we viewed our future. Even resilient. There was only one real mandatory – we had to be together. We were in love.

It was to be a small ceremony, with only thirty-five people invited. It was also to be in Johannesburg, where I lived, and a long way from my family or Gaynor's.

The consequence of this location was that yours truly was made responsible for doing most of the arranging. I've lived by the adage: "If you want to find the easy way to do anything, ask a lazy person". So the arrangements were simple – a church service, a reception at the home of my parents' friends, then Gaynor and I were off to Paris for our honeymoon.

The only exception to the smooth procedure was the matter of a non-Catholic marrying a Catholic. Yes, we had the obligatory meeting with the priest, which went badly. This was not the man who would perform the service, which was fortuitous.

In the process of the conversation he made certain statements I did not agree with, and being a young hot head who spoke out about what he believed, I told the priest what I thought of his proclamations. I wasn't rude, just adamant. His response was that if I really felt so strongly about it, his advice was that we shouldn't get married.

That was enough to make me see red, so I marched out, with Gaynor following me but not buying into the argument.

Wise she was, and still is. Outside, in the Mini I took a deep breath and started rationalising my anger.

"It's all okay," placated Gaynor.

"No it's not. What he said was just…I mean, who does he think he is?" I blustered.

"He's the priest," explained Gaynor. "He's saying what he's been trained to say."

I didn't buy that.

"Don't get married! Is that what he's been trained…!"

"No, no, no," said Gaynor, stroking my arm and my ego.

"Anyway," I continued, "Forget what he says, I want to marry you, and that's that!"

So I did and it was wonderful.

Several friends offered their help. Catering was taken care of by my mother's friend, Rae. Driving the bride was to be done by her husband, Donald, in his shiny new Jaguar. And my boss, Mike, offered his services as the official photographer.

There were no fancy invitations, no carefully selected songs or hymns, no menu for us to select, and no limo to worry about. The only concern I had was whether the marriage would work. After all, the wedding would last only a few hours, but the marriage…hopefully a lot longer.

It's interesting to look back from where I am now and consider those times. There we were, two young adults going along, inexperienced in most of the intricacies of life, heading into a partnership that felt right, but in fact, increased our vulnerability. Two heads may be better than one, provided those heads have enough combined wisdom and good sense. I'm not sure this described us accurately.

Nevertheless, on we sped, into our future together, unaware of what lay ahead, yet armed to overflowing with exuberance and excitement. We were in love, and love conquers all – or so the saying goes.

Saturday – the big day – arrived. My best friend John was to be my best man. He and I had enjoyed a few drinks and deep words the night before. We'd been brothers in arms on the rugby field and when we went spearfishing in some dangerous places. This wedding was another adventure – for me at least.

Dressed in our best suits and ties, we were first at the church. Friends and family began to arrive and sprinkle themselves sparsely among the pews. The priest arrived. But no bride (or bridesmaid). She did not arrive on time, or even ten minutes after the specified time. I knew she hadn't done a runner, because she had nowhere to run in Johannesburg. And her parents were there, waiting, like the rest of us.

You may be thinking this was probably Gaynor exercising her right as the bride to arrive only when she was good and ready, but this was not her style or the case. It was Donald, who lived only a kilometre or two away from the church, but had become hopelessly lost on the way.

Twenty minutes late, to the consternation of the bride and groom's parents and the priest, the service began. It should have been a scene in a movie. There was humour, drama, emotion and a strong sense of support from all the guests for this very young couple and their new commitment.

During the proceedings several things happened that stand out in my memory. I was startled when the priest unexpectedly splashed holy water on me. I'd had my eyes closed. Gaynor and her sister got the giggles because I was acting up. And once we were pronounced 'husband and wife' we turned to find everyone in the congregation in tears – men included. The tears were a mystery to me at the time, but I now believe it was the sincerest sign of their good wishes for our future.

Once the tears were wiped away and the congratulations offered we all headed off to the reception. It was in the spectacular garden of a beautiful home. Everyone was happy. People smiled and cameras clicked. Champagne flowed and food was consumed. We even danced to the music of a small band that miraculously appeared. It added to the mood of collective joy. This was fun!

Gaynor and I knew what time we needed to leave to arrive at our honeymoon destination, but that time ticked by with no departure on our part. We were having the time of our lives. If the rest of our time being husband and wife was to be anything like this, we were in for a good life.

Reluctantly, with the sun setting way off in the west, we climbed aboard…no, not a Boeing jet, heading for Paris, in France, but my little blue Mini, heading for Parys, a two horse town about two hours drive away.

I'd booked a hotel room for just one night, because Gaynor had to be back in Kimberley for school on Monday morning. Her students would be expecting her.

We arrived very late, had the night porter let us in, and found out the dining room and kitchen were closed.

At my age I needed constant feeding, and after all the excitement of the afternoon Gaynor was also peckish. So into the Mini we hopped and blasted off in search of food. We came back with a feast – placed a suitcase on the corner of the bed, and cracked open a bottle of not-French champagne.

There we sat smiling as we sipped champers and munched on hamburgers with the lot…and chips. It was perfect. Just the two of us. No high expectations. No airs and graces. Just the way we liked to live.

The conversation was filled with happy anecdotes about our special day. We were on our way as a couple.

After a leisurely breakfast on Sunday we were back in the Mini, heading west for Kimberley. Sunday night I stayed with my now in-laws, spoke with them late into the night about what a good time everyone had at the wedding, and laughed about how late everyone had left to go home. In the morning I waved Gaynor goodbye as she headed off to school.

That night I, in turn, took off for home, meaning that the first few weeks of our marriage we lived apart. There were no mobile phones, no facebook, no technology to connect us, but in a forty-seven year relationship that separation was only a blink of the eye.

Bent Thumb Thinking

If absence does make the heart grow fonder, perhaps all the time we spent apart at the start produced the glue that still binds us together today.

Recently I read a quote from a very happily married rock star by the name of Bono (I know you've heard of him) who said:

"Marriage is a grand madness. It's like jumping off a very tall building and discovering you can fly."

Too much thinking about whether or not to take the plunge would have grounded me, in that I would possibly not have jumped if I'd thought about all the consequences. So once again a little naivety worked for me. I'm so glad we took the leap together. It led to so many new experiences – like parenthood. But that's another story.

FOOTNOTE

This story is not meant to be anything more than an acknowledgement of the real blessing marriage has been in my life.

We started with almost nothing – three bread slicers and four fondue sets were among our wedding gifts, but a second-hand double bed and bed linen was the one we prized the most – and ended with everything.

This 'everything' has included a rock solid relationship, children and grandson who are a great source of joy, a strong shared faith and…well, what else is there that's really important?

Oh, the official photographs were ALL blank, so we have one picture of the day, thanks to best man John. Also memories, and they've been more than enough.

 "Best story ever! I can almost listen to your voice while I read this."
– Oscar Vega (Paraguay)

20

Marriage. A Risk Reward Analysis

What had I bought into when I got hitched? As with the diamond purchase, I went in blind and...

In the three-part story, 'Ring, Ask, Marry' I wrote an account of the activities leading up to and during the wedding that made Gaynor and I a permanent entity.

I also stated that I'd far sooner have a good marriage than a great wedding. Here's the audit.

The title 'A Risk, Reward Analysis' is completely tongue-in-cheek. Not for a moment have I ever truly analysed, in an accounting sense, the bottom line of our marriage.

What I have done here, however, is to reflect on the journey – through the good weather and the storms.

It seems to me that so many people, particularly today, make an analysis of this kind early on, and base it predominantly on the bottom line for themselves. More 'me' than 'us'.

I might have done the same thing initially, because the most powerful motive for marrying was to ensure I had time with someone who made me feel so much better when I was with her than when I wasn't.

Simple and simplistic perhaps, but the reality and result of the past forty-seven years has been spectacularly successful.

Before you stop reading, put off by the apparent arrogance of that statement, please know that I take no credit for how well married life has been for me – for us. I was ignorant stepping into the role of husband, and even more so becoming a father. So it seems that knowledge is not a prerequisite, certainly in a marriage.

What we did have was a friendship. That had been the start of our relationship. Gaynor was not interested in me at first – not in an emotional sense – even though I turned myself inside out trying to ignore what my heart was yelling to me every time I thought about her.

So we had spent hours, over many long months, talking. That's right! We spoke about our childhood, about travel, about lectures we'd endured, books and movies we'd liked and disliked, we even approached the very unlikely topic of poetry.

The outcome was that when we eventually held hands (don't laugh) there was more at play than just a fistful of fingers. We'd inadvertently revealed a fair amount about who we were and what we stood for to each other. And we liked what had been disclosed.

From a decidedly aimless existence as a student, who missed lectures and assignment deadlines on a regular basis, which was in my case a definite sign of being directionless and depressingly so, the slow blossoming of our relationship was a lifeline that kept me afloat.

Then there was Gaynor's family.

I saw and felt an enormous contrast between their values and those of my family. It's true that we judge ourselves – and those closest to us – with far greater stringency than we do those who are 'new' or not so close. And that's what I did back then.

There's a saying that explains why many people are so dissatisfied with themselves.

'We compare ourselves with others by what is worst about us and best about them'.

My family suffered this fate I'm sorry to say. There were all the failings, apparent faults and historic misunderstandings counting against them.

By contrast I was in love with Gaynor and her family. They were observed through undistorted and tainted lenses, because I knew nothing about them except what I saw there and then. So I judged them kindly. I even loved the little one-and-a-half horse town where she lived. She had friends who invited her to picnics and parties. When I was around they became my friends too.

Marriage was, I assumed, just a continuation of this great new life that had opened its arms and embraced me.

See, it was still a naïve view of reality. In Australia there's an old saying: 'She'll be right, mate'. I was a living example of that attitude, even though I'd never been there and had no idea I would one day live there.

Becoming parents, buying houses, moving cities and even countries have all been challenges, but never enough to knock us around unduly.

My recipe for a good marriage, therefore, is...

I don't have one. A higher hand guiding us, is my best attempt at an explanation. It's been the best experience of my life, in spite of occasional storms we've sailed through. And after the storm? Well, picking ourselves up, dusting ourselves off, and making up, present a certain sweetness – a sweetness that I haven't found in any other kind of relationship.

"Marriage works, but you have to make it."

That's what Gaynor's mother explained to her the night before our wedding, while I was having a quiet and contemplative drink with my Best Man, John. Happily I've been the beneficiary of that advice ever since.

Bent Thumb Thinking

So, by my reckoning, when all the beans are counted for "Mr. and Mrs. Crossan Inc." we've come out showing a profit every year. And that means it's been a good investment. No, great!

 "Your stories bring tears to my eyes and warm my heart."
— Julie Cliff

21

In a Dark World Focus on the Light

This is a short reflection on a circumstance I'm working through now. It is written to cast some light on a dark matter we are all eventually are confronted with – dying. My contention is that by discussing death we can gain perspective on life. And that is always a good thing.

In A Dark World, Focus On The Light.

What's the world coming to?
That's the question on so many minds. News from around the world is continually filled with wars, disasters, killings and refugees fleeing.

I have no simple answer to such a sweeping inquiry, but what I can do is answer this: What's my world coming to?

For each of us that is a far more pressing issue.

As outrageously self-centred as it may sound to some people, I've realised that my personal anxieties and attitudes over the years have next to no effect on global events.

On the other hand, I've learned that I can have an impact on a smaller scale – within my immediate community. And the big, wide world is made up of many, many little communities, is it not?

That's why, as individuals we should never give up on civilisation, or underestimate the role each of us plays in moulding it.

Let me explain...

I started this blog called Bent Thumb Thinking because I have a fascination about personal choices and the effects these have on our lives, and subsequently the lives of those around us.

Some choices we make consciously and rationally, like where we will spend our money – the local business or the multinational. Others we make as a result of our social conditioning and cultural background – the food we eat and the music we prefer. The third category is the result of our very individual thinking habits, and these choices tend to give us the same result every time.

It's this third type that fascinates me most, because habits are the actions that end up defining us, even though they seem to be beyond our control. They're the ingrained thought patterns – the well-worn tracks, or ruts – we fall into whenever we're confronted with a particular set of circumstances. The deeper they wear, the more difficult it is to steer out of them.

My "ruts" were tested severely a few years back. The circumstances challenged me to inspect my thought patterns in a way that I'd never done before. It presented the word "challenge" in capital letters.

I have an illness called Motor Neurone Disease, or ALS, that does not have a happy prognosis. Somewhere between one and three years after diagnosis is quoted as the average life expectancy.

In a word MND is terminal.

If you're not paying attention to where your life is heading, a diagnosis like that will change everything. Ironically the threat of death can make you more alive.

A new journey began, down roads and tracks I'd never negotiated before.

At first I was numb, but that didn't last long, and soon I advanced to a phase of philosophical questioning: Why me? Is it something I've done? Do I deserve this? These moved on to pragmatic queries. What's going to happen? Will I suffer? How long have I got?

As you can see, the questions were all about me. I allowed myself to focus on negatives – loss of co-ordination, withering muscles, dented sense of dignity, dribbling, eating with difficulty, choking when my mouth was full. I even thought about my own funeral, the songs they'd sing, the eulogy, and the people who'd come. What about those who might not bother?

Talk about dragging yourself into depression! That kind of thinking is a sure way to feel bad about life. It's a dark place.

It took time and some mental effort, but I moved into the third phase. What about all the people I love? How will they cope? In what ways will they be affected? What will their reactions and attitudes be to this predicament they find themselves in? Will they see me as a burden – an inconvenience?

It was a step forward, because I stopped being sorry for myself and started being sorry for them. They were the ones who had to put up with all the additional requirements of caring for me once I stopped being able to care for myself. Is there any way that I, in my predicament, can help them?

This led me to the next phase of thinking. It was the fourth step, and was probably the most interesting.

Entering this process I felt as though I was driving down a country road, and arriving at a T-junction. One way showed a steep descent into a dark and murky valley, the other was a seemingly endless climb into the mountains hidden by swirling mists.

In the valley, deep and dank, the sun would make no visit, but in the mountains, although the wind would blow, icy and unfriendly, I could imagine there would be sunny days ahead.

Life is all about forks in the road, and here I was with a major decision to make. Would I let the gravity of my predicament define me, through all the physical degeneration that MND brings with it, or would I use whatever time I had left to generate some meaning for my life?

My choice – do I go this way, or that? The high road or the low road? It was, and still is, my choice every morning.

I hadn't liked the lows I'd already been through in the past, so now I needed to make a wiser selection at this new crossroad and explore the other road.

Making that decision – to take the high road – has made no physical difference at all. I still struggle – to walk, to dress myself, to eat and to write, along with a list of other inconveniences. But there have been amazing metaphysical changes. Life now includes hope, purpose, value, richness, and all the unbankable, immeasurable blessings I'd not considered while trudging down the low road.

Happiness is a destination we have to drive towards every day, and the joy is not in reaching some special place on a metaphorical map, but in the active process of pursuing it. It's all in the striving.

This Bent Thumb Thinking blog is an exercise in counting

the many blessings I've already had on my road trip through life. The stories interested and amused my grandson on our real road trip when he was six, but they will also, I hope, provide him with a sense of the adventure life offers us all.

Hopefully they will show him that the way life looks depends on the lenses he wears – his perspective – whether he sees certain incidents as hardships only, or as opportunities to grow a little tougher and a little wiser.

Like everyone, I've experienced tough times in my life. There have been plenty of things people have done to me or said to me that have hurt. They've even left scars. But I believe in a simple credo:

Your focus will define you, so remember the good times, and look with hope to the future. Choose to follow the light.

PS: In December, 2015 it was SIX years since I was diagnosed, so I'm ahead of the average by several years. Was that good luck or the road I chose? Perhaps a bit of both.

 "Graham, we admire your tenacity, resilience and perspective. May God bless you on your journey to the light ..."
– Peter McKenna

22

Immature Immigration Part 1

Looking back on one's life can provide a picture of a person you've completely forgotten. In some cases it can be a pleasing revelation, whilst in others, it's a shock to realise just what you were like way back when...

This is a story about immigration. Considering how often the word "immigration" is in the news these days, and most often in a negative context, this story provides a contrast that provides a glimpse of what half a century of time has done to the process – and the prospects.

Oh for the innocent old days!

I had been a very bad university student. One who almost never got my assignments done on time, and even worse, there were many I didn't get done at all.

But when I actually got a job in advertising I was a changed person. I was almost the first at work in the morning and the last person out of the door at night. Colleagues who read this will disagree, but by way of comparison to my days on campus, this is how it felt to me.

The difference was I'd found something I loved to do, which was to write.

Two years in this exciting career went by and I'd been a sponge, soaking up all the information I could on an industry I'd known nothing about until I was in it.

I was told that the mecca of advertising was the USA.

"If that's the case, what am I doing here in Johannesburg?"

As presumptuous as it sounds, I decided after just two years, that, small fish I might be, but I needed to be in a bigger pond. The USA was the place for me.

I started making enquiries and found out from the US embassy that my chances of emigrating were slim. to say the least. In fact I was told that the category I fitted into was only one or two categories above cats and dogs going with their owners.

Being in my early twenties meant I was easily daunted, but not defeated, so I became momentarily disillusioned. But, I was working with a guy, another writer about my age, called Ron. He was Canadian.

When I told him about this he made the obvious suggestion.

"Why don't you go to Canada first? Half the people who end up in the USA started off in Canada."

I had no idea about the legalities of immigrating to Canada.

"Well how do you do that?" I asked. The answer was glaringly obvious.

"Phone the Canadian embassy – and by the way, my dad is in advertising in Montreal, so if you can get there I'm sure he'll be able to help you find a job."

Perfect! I phoned the Canadian attaché, because they didn't have an embassy in South Africa. I spoke to a lady, who told me that the quota for immigrants to Canada for that year and the next was full, so my chances of being accepted were no good for at least two years.

"However," she explained, "the procedure you would need to follow is to go to the nearest Canadian embassy – that's in Addis Ababa – and fill in all the relevant forms. Then you submit them and in around six months you'll be contacted for an interview. So you'd have to fly back there for that. And in about another six months you'll be notified about whether you've been successful."

I groaned. Audibly.

"But you can also go to London if that suits you better," she chirped quite cheerfully.

"Oh no!" I now whined. "That's very disappointing. I don't know if I can wait that long."

It was a weird thing to say, on reflection, but it elicited an equally weird response. It was a response delivered in a low, secretive tone.

"Strictly off the record, what you could do – even though you can't tell anyone I suggested this – is go to Canada on holiday, and while you're there, apply for immigration. Some people have got in that way."

My spirits soared. I said thanks very much, put the phone down and thought.

"That's what I'll do. She must know that's the best way to go."

I went home and told Gaynor. Up to then I hadn't thought at all about the mechanics of how we were going to get there or how much money it would cost.

At this point I have a confession to make. Confessing, I am told, can be very therapeutic for the soul.

You see, by then Gaynor had already been overseas, spending an amazing year in America as an exchange student. I was wracked with jealousy, and this escapade would cure the green fog that descended whenever she spoke of her travels.

So the planning proceeded. With some help from my friend

Ron, I organised to fly to Montreal via England, staying for a week with a friend of mine from university. He was a Rhodes Scholar at Oxford, so what better reason could one have to visit that iconic place than to catch up with an old drinking buddy.

Gaynor and I sold everything we owned. Everything, that is, that anyone would give us money for. We ended up with just enough money for one and a half airline tickets. The plan was that Gaynor and our son, who was not even a year-old, would stay with my parents until I got a job in advertising over there and send her the money to buy the rest of her ticket.

"If you had no money for Gaynor's ticket, how did you have enough money to make a stop over in the UK?" I hear you ask.

My answer, as I sit here writing this account, is that my young adult brain just managed to ignore the question. I was going overseas! That was my focus.

Off I went. I flew KLM to Amsterdam and then on to London. My friend met me at Heathrow and on we travelled by train to Oxford. I had a wonderful time for a week catching up. We hadn't seen each other for a few years. We sampled the beer and the pickled onions and cheese from Ploughman's Lunch in Oxford.

Oh, I did visit the Bodlean Library, and walked through the wonderful academic precinct in awe of its place in history. But the beer, sadly, was more of a focal point. Give me a break. I was young and immature. I now concede that I was.

At the end of the week I flew back to Holland and from Schiphol airport I took the flight to Montreal.

Half way across the Atlantic I started thinking ahead, to Montreal, my new home – sorry, our new home.

I knew nothing much about it. Somehow I'd only considered it a short-term stopover on my way to New York.

And then I wondered about who was going to meet me at the airport. I had the address of Ron's parents, but would I need to take a taxi? Hmm!

Only then did my brain really consider the reality of what awaited me.

"I should really have been in touch with them…at least to confirm that they're expecting me," I pondered.

When you're twenty-five it's one of those details that somehow is not part of your thinking. It certainly wasn't a part of mine.

I worried a bit about whether they were expecting me. I couldn't remember if Ron had said he had contacted his parents. He did tell me he was going to. Didn't he?

The plane landed and I lined up in the queue for immigration with my cabin bag, my small suitcase of clothes and my high hopes of success.

Eventually I was called forward. The immigration officer looked at my passport and the declaration sheet I'd filled out. After a few seconds of perusing these, he spoke to somebody on the phone. Then he turned his attention back on me.

"Mr Crossan, go to door number five over there. Someone will just clarify a few details."

I had no idea what was going to happen, but I said yes okay, and went in through the door marked number five.

Inside was a woman in a uniform, sitting at a desk. She looked very serious.

"Please sit. I have a few questions."

This officer proceeded to interrogate me. In my naivety, I answered without thinking too carefully. Just the truth. Then she asked the crunch question.

"Are you here on holiday?"

"Oh yes. And I'm looking forward to seeing this beautiful country," I enthused.

"How long will you be here?"

This caught me off guard. I hadn't thought about being asked that question. I didn't want to make my stay sound too short. But, then again, I couldn't make it too long either. So I made up a number.

"Uh, six months. Umm! Yeah, six months."

The woman looked at me for a long moment, then she spoke.

"That's nice. And where will you be going?"

That was another tricky question. I realise it now, but at the time it seemed perfectly innocuous. This Canadian official was just interested in ensuring my visit was enjoyable, wasn't she?

I explained that I'd be staying in Montreal for much of the time.

"Where will you be staying?"

That was easy to answer, although my confident voice was tinged with concern. I hoped my hosts knew I'd be residing with them.

"Oh! With Mr and Mrs K. Their son is a good friend of mine."

"And what about the rest of the time?

"We're planning to do a bit of travelling. I'm not sure what they have in mind."

"How much money do you have with you, Mr Crossan?"

This was the crunch question. In today's terms it would be about two hundred dollars. For six months. Even I knew it sounded completely unrealistic.

The immigration officer paused a moment and then delivered the news I didn't want to hear.

"You know you're not allowed to work while you're here."

"Umm! Yes. Yes, I do."

I did know definitely now. However, the fact that I now knew didn't mean I'd dispelled every thought of finding a job.

The interview continued, ending with a question that had me feeling even more uncomfortable than all the others.

"Would you mind if I called Mr K?"

A thought flashed through my mind as we looked at each other – this could be very awkward. For a start I didn't know whether Mr K would even recognise my name. He might not even be expecting me. And even if he did, I had no idea what his reaction might be to a phone call from an officer in the immigration department.

I read out the number and she dialled. We both waited.

Now imagine this picture: I can only hear what she is saying and have no idea how my friend's father is responding.

"Hello. Am I speaking to Mr K?"

Silence – for me.

She proceeded to tell him who she was and where she was ringing from.

"I have a gentleman here by the name of Graham Crossan. Do you know him?"

Silence again – for me.

"Mr. Crossan tells me he will be staying with you? Is that correct?"

More silence, as she listened to what he was saying. I could not hear a word.

After several more questions and answers, she put her hand over the mouthpiece of the phone and asked me a question. It sent a shiver down my spine.

"Would you like to speak to Mr K?"

By now I wanted to slide under the carpet and disappear. I'd never talked with the man before and didn't know him from Adam. But I had no choice – I had to say…

"Oh, yes, please. I'd love to."

She handed me the handpiece, which I took with shaking hands. In the friendliest voice I could contrive at the time I spoke to Mr K for the very first time.

"MR. K! How are you? It's so nice to talk to you."

His reaction was totally unexpected.

"What the hell are those miserable, officious uniformed (exact words forgotten, but they were not complimentary) doing to you?"

Mr K was incensed that I was being given a hard time. I later learned that he was very anti-establishment and hated the sight of a uniform.

Anyway he said the magic words – that they were expecting me.

"Would you like me to pick you up at the airport?"

I said I would love him to and we made arrangements about where to meet. I put the phone down and that was that.

The lady who had regarded me so suspiciously before the phone call, stamped my passport. I was in Canada with a six-month visa. As I walked out the door she reminded me that I was not allowed to work in Canada on a Visitor's Visa. I said, "Oh yes I do."

Mr K collected me and we went home. I stayed with them for the next two weeks, listening to Bob Dylan for the very first time. "The Times They Are A Changing" rang in my head for weeks. This was courtesy of the record player in Ron's bedroom, where I was sleeping.

All I needed now was Gaynor. For that to happen all I needed was what I'd been told I couldn't have – a job.

In the next story I'll reveal how our little family was reunited – and grew by one – in beautiful Quebec.

 "I'm crying with laughter over your amazing lack of proper preparation and yet it somehow works out."

– James Parsons

23

Immature Immigration Part 2

Landing in a new country is not the end, nor the beginning of the end. It's only the end of the beginning of immigration.

Let's face it, many of the things we do in life we don't think through before doing them.

As a matter of fact, if we did, we wouldn't get half as many things done as we've managed to. That goes for you as well as for me.

I know that a lot of the best things I've ever done happened on the spur of the moment, or without thinking them through. That's how I met my wife. That's how I had my children. That's how I got jobs and that's how I ended up in Australia – without thinking the consequences through all that carefully.

So there I was in Canada, in the beautiful city of Montreal. All I needed now was to get Gaynor and my eight-month-old son back with me.

I know that sounds totally selfish, and if you're thinking that way, you're probably quite right, because, up to that point I'd only thought about myself in terms of making this amazing trip. It was simply to tick off on my wish list the desire to travel overseas.

In order to get the two of them over to Montreal I had to buy a second airline ticket. For that I needed money. And to get money I had to work for it, which meant finding a job.

Mr K was wonderful, because he and his wife gave me accommodation for two weeks or so. In addition, Mr K made a number of phone calls to see if there was anyone in his circle of business acquaintances who was looking for a junior copywriter. That's what I was, even though I had a much higher opinion of myself.

The problem was that, unbeknown to me, Canada was going through a recession at that particular time. This meant few industries were taking on more staff. In fact, the advertising industry was getting rid of staff.

In spite of this, the time I spent in Montreal benefitted me in ways I didn't expect and didn't even realise until some years later.

But, first things first. To find myself a job I had a number of interviews and even went to Toronto and back twice. My mode of transport was one I'd honed during my time in compulsory military service five years earlier.

Hitchhiking around Canada was, in itself, an adventure, because people who pick up hitchhikers seemed at that time to fall into two categories. The first was people who just wanted to be helpful, which I was grateful for. The other was people who wanted somebody to talk to about their issues. I have to say that in that second category I had some hair-raising conversations with drivers who decided that, having offered me a lift, they were entitled to earbash me for the duration of the trip. I was stuck in their car, so there was no escape.

It took about a month for me to find a job. This turned out to be the worst job I've ever had, but it taught me some fundamental lessons.

At the end of the first month working there I was handed a pay packet and responded in a way that surprised the person doing the handing out.

"Oh! But this isn't for me. The name on the envelope isn't mine."

The reply was equally baffling.

"That's your pay. Don't worry about it – that's definitely yours."

"Oh! OK, thanks. Thanks a lot."

I walked off without a second thought.

Now, it's obvious that I was just not thinking clearly. The idea of accepting a pay packet with someone else's name may have surprised you, but didn't really strike me as odd. After all, I was in a strange country, living in a strange city, surrounded by people, speaking a strange language. This seemed to be just another odd custom.

I just took it all for granted, and that was that.

Within another month I had enough money to send to Gaynor for purchasing the second airline ticket. She arrived three months after I got there with a baby boy who was, it seemed, twice the size he'd been the last time I saw him. Simon was now a little plump fellow, thanks, I'm sure, to my mother's cooking and her insistence (even in my life) that food was the answer to every problem.

I'd also moved into an apartment with the help of Mrs K, who, I think, had worked out that if she didn't do something to get me out of their house I was going to be there permanently. It was just so comfortable and, somehow, I'd failed to consider that I might be some kind of imposition.

Gaynor, Simon and I lived in Westmount, which was the English section of Montreal. We lived in an apartment where all the furniture, including couches and lounge chairs, was painted with white, yellow and red household paint – even the cushions. It was very clean but felt very weird.

Culturally this life was so different from anything we had experienced before. Quebec was fiercely French at that time. We had armoured cars in the streets, protesters in front of Parliament House, scuffles with the police, a British diplomat kidnapped and a Quebec politician shot. But for all that, we had a wonderful time.

We met some amazing people, one of whom was Khan-Tineta Hahn, a Mohawk Indian woman who was an activist, looking for better conditions for her people. She told us stories of life on the reservation that was somewhat reminiscent of life for many people in South Africa.

We were invited to Khan-Tineta's birthday party and I had a most unusual introduction to one of her friends.

"Graham, I'd like you to meet my friend John."

In truth I don't remember his name, so I've called him John.

"Hello John."

"How ya doin', Grey-me."

"John, have a look at Graham. What can you see?"

Kahn-Tineta asked this as she eye-balled me. John, who was also a Mohawk, leaned deep into my personal space and inspected my face carefully.

"He's scared."

"Huh!"

That was my intelligent response. John continued.

"Drinks too much milk."

I'd never had an introduction like that before, and I've never had one since. It was very uncomfortable, although I realised immediately that they were not doing anything deliberately to make me feel bad. It was a cultural thing.

"What do you mean, I'm scared. And what's this about drinking too much milk?"

"Tell him, John."

John proceeded to explain that in their culture adults did not partake of any dairy products, particularly milk. It was just not done.

I was curious and asked for some explanation.

"It's simple buddy. Have you ever seen a bull sucking on a cow's teat?"

What? That was a weird question. I shook my head and John went on.

"That's because milk is made for babies, and it's no good for adults. Makes you scared like a baby."

You learn something new every day, I thought. I stored up this information and for at least a month I avoided milk diligently. But that was enough time for me to decide I was not a bull, so the example didn't apply to me.

We loved living in Montreal.

Occasionally on Sunday mornings we'd walk down to a bridge near the St Lawrence River, where a farmers' market was held. We marvelled at the fresh produce, particularly the apples, which had a redness and juiciness we'd not encountered anywhere before.

We travelled on trains and buses exploring the beautiful city of Montreal and twice left town, when a work colleague lent us his car.

The first time was to travel to a wedding in Cincinnati, Ohio. It was summer and the occasion was exciting, particularly for Gaynor.

After high school Gaynor had spent a year in that city as an exchange student, living with a host family. Her American 'sister' was now getting married and she was part of the bridal party.

This was my first time in the USA, so I was mildly awestruck. I had big Bob – pronounced Baab – assigned to look after me. My assessment of the USA: lovely people, but lousy beer. That was the yardstick I used for measuring many things back then. Beer.

The other road trip was to Quebec City, a beautiful historic town. We went there with my friend Ron, who'd returned from his travels. It was later in the year and autumn was in full swing.

After spending a few hours sightseeing in Quebec City, oohing and aahing at the old citadel and fortifications, we knew we needed to find accommodation for the night. Being desperately poor we decided to travel a fair way out of town to find cheaper rates.

We drove and drove, passing village after village, but not stopping. What we did notice was that in each village the local hotel had a neon sign flashing. Everyone had the same message – one we could read, but did not understand.

It said 'Le Spectac'.

We asked resident Canadian, Ron, what this was. His answer created a number of alternative mental pictures. None were good.

"It's just a kind of floor show. They run on Friday and Saturday night. I guess out here it's probably just the proprietor's daughter doing a dance on the bar counter."

When we finally did stop, the floorshow had finished, so we never did get to see what it really was. It was only a small deficit in our cultural induction to life in rural Quebec.

The next day was way more significant. In the morning we headed further north and slowly, as the miles ticked by, we watched the trees become shorter and shorter. We were moving closer to the tundra region. Then we veered south-west, following a river that wound endlessly through the hills.

As we travelled, our jaws dropped further and further. The scenery came alive. It was spectacular. For as far as we could see, the world was covered in maple trees, painted with a brilliant palettes of autumn shades – from russet red to infinite hues of brown and gold and yellow.

On and on it went, this painted pathway of a road. Around bends, over hills and into valleys. For over an hour the world was alight and alive, showing off just how much more impressive the real thing is to any photographic reproduction.

This was our 'Le Spectac'.

Our baby son turned one in Montreal. He had grown so much. Not that interested in speaking, Simon was more inclined to movement. Having crawled at five months, walked at eight months, he now proved to be a consummate acrobat and escape artist.

Often, early in the mornings when we woke up, we could hear him playing with his toys in his bedroom. Our concern was that these were toys that had been left on the floor the night before when we put him to bed in his high-sided cot.

The question was this – how did he get from the cot to the floor?

We were afraid of the answer, and decided the way to deal with this was not so much to try keeping him in the cot, but rather to make sure that if he fell out, it was not too far to fall. So we proceeded to leave the cot side down at night.

It worked. He climbed out and never fell. Not that we know of, anyway.

For his birthday we gave him what proved to be his favourite toy. No, we didn't buy it from a toy store, because it was a feeding chair.

The first night, Gaynor sat him in the chair, then placed his food on the little tables in front of him. He got some of the food in him, but most of the food on him.

Then he proceeded to push the bowl off the table section. That was when the fun began in earnest. While we mindlessly watched 'Rowan and Martin's Laugh-in' on TV in black and white, with Lily Tomlin doing her switchboard operator routine, Simon was deeply involved in exploring the power of gravity.

He managed to climb out of the seat and onto the little table. Then he rotated his legs to the front, while hanging onto the outer edge of the table. After a few seconds he decided it was time to let go.

Luckily he was tall for his age and the feeding chair was short. He slid off, bumped his chin on the edge of the table and landed on the floor. We looked up when he screamed, but it was a scream of frustration, not pain.

We then watched with amazement – sorry Lily – as he climbed back into the chair and looked as pleased as punch when he was sitting up there again. The process was repeated, but this time he held on to the inner edge of the table and let himself down slowly. It was not an instant success, but the yells got less audible and the smile on his face became broader as he mastered this process.

In a matter of fifteen minutes he'd turned the feeding chair into a jungle gym, and it remained that for as long as we lived there.

Life in those days was difficult from a financial point of view. It was also hard working for companies who did not operate in a way that I had been taught. So I was under pressure, even though I had now been working in my chosen profession for a full two and a half years. I say that with my tongue firmly in my cheek because, looking back, I realise that I knew very little. A novice is what I was, although I didn't feel that way then.

We also had the issue of immigration to deal with. Countless telephone conversations eventually succeeded in securing an appointment with the Department of Immigration. I was told I needed to bring my wife with me.

This sounded like a bonus because, in my estimation, Gaynor was far more persuasive about international affairs than me.

On the appointed day the three of us arrived at the offices, filled out the forms handed to us and stood waiting to be called. We were then summoned separately. I was sent into an office where a middle-aged French man with grey hair and glasses proceeded to ask me a number of seemingly innocuous questions.

These included facts about our financial situation. I tried to remember what I'd said to the airport staff months earlier and decided to stick close to that story if I could.

When we'd finished, the officer asked me to wait there. He went off and fetched Gaynor, sat her down next to me, organised a sweet biscuit for Simon, and began to ask her the same questions I'd answered.

Gaynor's answers regarding our finances turned my face pale. They seemed to contradict what I had said in every detail. In particular, the amount of money we professed to have at our disposal was vastly different. I'd exaggerated low, and Gaynor had gone high.

The man questioning us smiled and eventually spoke to Gaynor.

"Do you know how much money your husband says you have? It is not what you say."

Gaynor looked at him, then at me and back at him, crestfallen.

"Do you have some money your husband does not know about?"

This was obviously a rhetorical question because he laughed quietly and said something that was reassuring.

"Madam, you do not have to make stories for me. I can see that you and your baby are beautiful, so I want to make it easy for you."

With that, he helped us fill in more forms and reassured us that they would be processed promptly.

We left there laughing nervously and wondering just how this would all turn out. Would it be a disaster, in spite of what the kind-hearted Frenchman had said.

A month later we had wonderful news.

However, this was news of a different nature. Gaynor was pregnant again. Good news, but not good timing. We were struggling already, but then again, our whole three years of married life had been a struggle. This was a blessing wrapped up in a challenge. At the start we didn't know the extent of either of these.

Gaynor went through normal processes of seeing a doctor and then a specialist paediatrician quite regularly. Within a couple of weeks, when I arrived home from work, I found her distraught.

"What's the matter?"

This wasn't the resilient person I was used to, but I was yet to find out the reason.

"I saw the specialist today. He told me there's a fifty-fifty chance there'll be complications with the baby. Serious problems."

I needed more information.

Ironically, whilst we are compatible in every other aspect, Gaynor and I have incompatible blood. This had been something of a problem with the first pregnancy, but now it threatened to be disastrous.

"What do they say you should do?"

Gaynor's answer was terse.

"It's not me, it's us."

I took that rebuke on the chin. We were in the predicament together.

"Ok. What did they say we should do?"

"The advice is to terminate the pregnancy."

I thought carefully before asking the next question. This can happen when you've already been reprimanded.

"Wow! That's radical. How do you feel about that?"

Gaynor, who is no shrinking violet, did have tears in her eyes when she answered, but the answer was one of defiance.

"I don't want to do that. What about you?"

I had nothing like the fortitude of my wife, so answered in a way that was correct, but in no way was taking full responsibility.

"Well, the thing is, I'm not pregnant. So I can have an opinion, but it doesn't affect me physically like it does you."

She nodded. That was it.

We had agreed and I am so grateful we did. Now it was a matter of working out how to ensure the best medical care for Gaynor and the fifty-fifty baby. The way forward was definitely not clear, but from that moment there was no more fretting.

Isn't it amazing how things work out – most often for the good. That's always been my experience anyway.

Within a matter of weeks, while at work, I received a phone call from South Africa. It was my old boss.

"Howzit Graham?"

"Mike? Is that you, Mike?"

It was. He explained that the phone call was prompted by information he'd received that we were doing it tough in Canada.

"How'd you like to have your old job back?"

I thought for a while. Actually it was a millisecond before I answered

"Man, I'd love it. But how do we get back to South Africa? I've got no money."

We worked out all the details there and then. It was a wonderful solution to most of the problems we were facing.

Early in December of 1970 we boarded a plane bound for England, where we stopped over for a visit to Oxford University. We had no money, but managed a holiday anyway.

Of all the foods available in England, the only thing Gaynor wanted to eat was fish and chips. On the other hand, Simon, in the pubs and eating places we frequented, took a fancy to pickled onions and cheese. A one-year-old liking pickled onions?

Arriving back in Johannesburg was not altogether plain sailing. We had to set up house again. I had no car and all the items we'd sold, like a bed and a fridge and all those other essentials, now had to be re-purchased.

This we managed to do with painful slowness. Don't forget, I'd only been in my profession three years.

Was it all worthwhile?

The hardship of that time away had pushed the two of us together. Gaynor and I had suffered and survived by joining forces – by working together. So our relationship had grown immeasurably.

And my career was set to step up a notch. At work, within weeks, I was confronted with a question that came up several times,

"Who did you work for over there? You've learned so much while you've been away."

These questioners had me confused, because both jobs in Montreal had been such a challenge. The questions did get me thinking. What had I learned? Had anyone actually taught me anything about my craft? After some consideration I realised what had probably happened.

The lack of work systems and professional thinking in the agencies in Montreal had forced me to question what I'd already been taught.

"Why do I do things this way? How come I automatically follow a process that these new companies don't?"

I realised that my mentors in Johannesburg knew what they were doing, and they'd indoctrinated me in the ways they worked. The weird thing was that, all the while that I'd been learning them, my awareness was only about the process, not the purpose. University hadn't worked for me, but these methods did.

This may sound very Irish, but what had happened can best be explained like this:

We don't know what we don't know, but more importantly, we don't always know what we do know.

The greatest gift we brought back from our brief encounter with this first immigration attempt, however, was delivered five months after our arrival. That fifty-fifty chance was now a perfectly formed baby girl.

I'm happy to say that our baby daughter is now a woman named Ande, and an amazing one at that.

Life is a risky business. I look back at some of the most wonderful things that have ever happened in my life and smile. What if I hadn't trusted that things would all work out for the good?

How much poorer my life would have been without these things – the people, the children, the places. Oh, and the scars.

 "Very enjoyable read, full of life, fun and drama, joy and heartache."
– David Kimpton

24

A Porcelain Picture of Hope

How precious are children to their parents? In my case they are the most precious part of my life. Both of them were easily conceived, but a lot harder to deliver.

In the case of Ande there were serious concerns about whether she would survive or not. In fact, the initial medical advice was that there was a fifty-fifty chance of birth defects, or worse, when the time came.

Miraculously those doctors were proved wrong. A beautiful light entered our world, although it was not an auspicious beginning. She had a complete blood transfusion at birth and remained in hospital for longer than was normal. The fact that she did survive brought not only relief to us, but a joy above the average.

As she grew, the trauma of her first few days receded and she flourished.

When I see her now, this tall, self-assured and highly competent woman, it's hard for me to bring back pictures of when she was a little girl. At the age of two the first thing you noticed was a pair of the biggest, bluest eyes, surrounded by a certain solemnness that suggested there'd been a serious struggle in the past for her. It belied the woman she was destined to grow into.

Today that little girl is only a dim memory. But when I wander in our back garden there's something that brings all the confusion, all the joy, all the marvellous mystery of being the father of a girl child flooding back.

It's a porcelain doll.

Sitting on an old garden table is a little pottery girl. She's wearing a bonnet, has solemn blue eyes, and with her dress of many colours gathered around her, she sits solidly on the ground.

The figurine is the result of an art lesson Ande had in high school. I'm quite sure she was not consciously doing a self-portrait at the time. In fact, the porcelain person looks nothing like the real child I refer to. But every time I see the doll it reminds me so strongly of that solemn little girl seated on the floor of our family home in Cape Town so long ago.

The porcelain doll is, in my mind, a perfect metaphor for real life – the life of my little girl who's grown. Out in the garden, seated in silence, it weathers the storms, the hot sun in summer, and whatever life chooses to throw at it.

In its travels, from one house to the next, across oceans and over the years, it's starting to show a bit of wear. If you look carefully, with critical eyes, you'll notice that there are chips and abrasions starting to appear. But if you look with loving eyes you will see the essence of the child. Still shining brightly.

It is, for me, a symbol of hope in a very uncertain world.

25

The Return

This is something I wrote about three years ago as a result of a journey my wife and I made to retrace some long ago parts of our lives. My journey back to the boarding school I'd attended for five formative years is the subject here. It's written as a final school essay – a little more formal than the style I'm used to.

The Return

The effect of certain events in our lives can be deceptively powerful. Their gravity can cut through decades of neglect to expose the deepest emotions about a phase of our life we presumed had been left well and truly behind. Buried.

Why?

Why is it that certain memories, when they do bubble up, often at the most inappropriate time, are so tactile and tender that they throw us off balance, leaving us struggling to stay composed.

This was my first visit in almost half a century. I was returning to the school where five important developing years of my life had been spent, isolated from family, divorced from the nurturing of normal home life, learning the lessons all teenage boys encounter, but without the convention of close parental guidance – a father who sits you down, a mother who implicitly understands.

No school can offer those, but this school had been good to me and for me in everything it could provide. I knew at the time of being a scholar there that it was a good school, but I didn't know how good. I do know now, but at the time of leaving I'd walked away wanting nothing more to do with the place.

Why?

In April 2012 my wife and I spent a morning being generously shown around St. Andrews College, Grahamstown – the school of my youth. It was a morning of revelation and reflection.

What was revealed was a campus of amazing beauty and historical significance set in a town that by coincidence bears my first name. I saw it this time, and for the first time, through adult eyes, recognising the grandeur of the old stone buildings, the vast interconnected playing fields and the beautifully kept gardens.

But now there was another dimension – something altogether new.

As I walked around the school grounds it seemed as if I remembered every nook and cranny that remains after all these years, each part of it etched indelibly on a young and eager mind. Every pathway, every alleyway, every blade of grass had been part of the race I ran each and every day through those five years of school.

When I was a student I loved to run. In the early years it was to keep one step ahead of any lurking seniors, who could spell trouble for a first or second year student, but later I ran because I found that I was quite good at it. Moving swiftly from point to point was more important back then than enjoying the journey. The stopwatch ruled over my deeper emotions – my heart. Fast was a victory, slow a defeat.

Our tour of the school this time was done at a more leisurely pace. Geriatric I am not, but at my age the world has slowed considerably. And as we walked around what we once referred so glibly to as "College" I experienced an overwhelming sense of conflict.

I'd left in a hurry, with never a backward glance. At the end of five years I was looking forward to forging a life of freedom and doing what I, yes, what I, wanted to do, replacing forever the highly regulated life of a boarder in a school steeped in other people's traditions. From the time you woke as a student, until the lights went out each night, someone else was in command. Even as a prefect, where there were many more liberties, the chain of command still dragged annoyingly, inhibiting any sense of real personal freedom for me.

Perhaps it was no surprise to my teachers then that when the final exam was completed I was off, running again, as I had done all summer through athletics, and that winter wearing our rugby colours with pride.

Was I running away when I left, or merely moving on, as every student needs to do?

As it happened I was off to do military service, where personal freedom was reduced to zero and restrictions were enforced with a rigour that I'd never experienced before, even as a boarder. But my eyes were still focussed on the future, rather than those "left behind" school days and the life lessons they'd taught me with tacit subtlety.

From there the years unfolded in a series of spirals that sent me following the tide of the times – still running – across South Africa, to North America and later Australia, until that run was reduced to a slow amble around Espin, Kettlewell, the Chapel and all the other familiar College landmarks.

The profound realisation for me, after all the years of wrestling the world and struggling through the challenges life places before all of us, was that, happily, the school and I have both survived. In fact, we've flourished, each in our own way. Though we've taken our separate paths, it was I who was more moved by the constancy of life as it confronted me in the school grounds that gentle autumn morning.

The emotion I felt on returning was strong enough to surprise me. Why did I choke up when I was shown through my old house? Why did my heart jump as I stepped through the grand wooden doors of a deserted chapel?

What was so moving about standing on the green grass of Lower field with not a soul in the stands this time? No cheers, no nerves, no opponents waiting to engage in battle on the rugby field. How come the tuck shop tugged at my heart this time, rather than my belly? And did I really hear the echo of legendary maths master, Drac Lucas' thunderous voice scolding some inattentive scholar?

Since that day I've pondered. Why did I feel all those strong emotions? Why did tears embarrass me as they welled up uncontrollably? And is it only me who's experienced this response on returning?

I believe my reactions were those of a prodigal son of sorts, who'd left without a thought about just what St. Andrews had meant in my life – the inheritance it had handed me so willingly. Until decades had passed I'd never bothered to stop long enough in my headlong rush to consider the moral values, the social perspectives, the personal associations and the enormous privilege the institution had bestowed on me. These gifts were given, not just because my parents had paid a fee for them, but because an endless progression of people over the years had dedicated themselves to making these assets available to each and every student who passes through the school. Time has taught me that, in every situation, some people grab as much as they can manage, others pass by without even knowing what they've missed.

Selfish may be too strong a word to describe my attitude as a College boy. More accurate may be to say I was unaware at the time of all the gifts on offer. Some I understood and appreciated, such as an English teacher called Mr. Sutherland who lit a fire in me for writing. Thanks to him I've made a career as a writer. I wept with sadness and gratitude when I heard of his death. By then I was already a man with school aged children. The sadness stemmed from never having thanked him personally for the safety he'd provided for me to test my wings with words in his classes, and the gratitude was for him being an encourager to a boy uncertain of his worth. And sport had rewarded me immensely, allowing me to remodel my self-esteem after years of anguish, by representing a team, and a tribe, on playing fields where winning was important, but participating was far more.

There was even Chapel every Sunday, which provided for me a sense of something worthwhile when I felt so much else in my life was not. It was a place where I felt that if there was a God then the most likely place He'd be was there. And in my child's heart I suppose that was a comfort, so I attended without complaining – in fact with a certain relish.

Many of the other offerings provided by the school I dismissed, perhaps because they were too intangible for me to understand. The history of the institution, the generosity of the old boy network, the investment in resources both academic, artistic and recreational – these never registered on my gauge of importance.

Coming back to school brought my life's journey into stark relief. Here I was, face to face with the surroundings and the struggles of the teenager I had been, living away from home, and having to fend for himself. They were good times, but they were not easy times.

Struggle can make you strong, but the cuts and abrasions of growing up leave permanent scars. For the most part they play no negative role in later life, but every now and then, especially as the years move on, the pains of the past return to remind us of where we've come from and what we've lived through. There's a certain wisdom just in knowing that.

In the biblical story the prodigal son returns to his father's home after squandering the inheritance lovingly given to him. His return is cause for joy and celebration. In my case I was returning to a mother of sorts – an alma mater – which the dictionary defines as a bounteous mother. How appropriate. While not a perfect metaphorical fit, it is fit for consideration. After all, the inheritance which I had never fully accepted, in spite of it being offered to me and every student who passes through the school, is not too often thought of as that – an inheritance.

So in this regard the return was the final lesson in this particular circle of my life. Complete. Arriving back at the beginning. Knowing now why the journey was taken in the first place.

I never was a fast student, but I generally got there in the end. This has been no different.

The inheritance is now acknowledged and accepted. Thank you mother of my youth. Thank you St. Andrews College, Grahamstown. Thank you all who have contributed to this gift.

 "Graham, I really enjoyed reading this as you have managed to encapsulate what most of us feel."

– Adrian Van Selm (South Africa)

26

We Began To Talk Again

This is not a story, but an essay, so it's a departure from the other Bent Thumb Thinking fare. It was written some time ago when I was in a sentimental frame of mind. Whilst partly biographical, it does express a truth about all relationships.

We Began To Talk Again

It was early in the Spring that we began talking. Our conversations had, for some time, been focussed more on the humdrum aspects of life than on our dreams, or fears, for the future.

That's the great difficulty of marriage, or of any longstanding relationship, for that matter. Whether you are husband and wife, two old friends, or a master and dog, eventually you grow to know the thoughts of the other without the need for conversation.

It's a sort of comfort, in a way, not having to speak, to express, to grapple with words and thoughts, and air them for someone else to hear.

Communication had become a struggle. It always had been for me. My inclination, especially in my younger years, was more towards thought than expression. Something way back in my childhood, perhaps, contrived to silence me. So the thought of speaking was far less appealing than just sitting in the sun like some lizard and watching the world go by, entertaining my own thoughts and observations.

But that changed. Mysteriously, magically, that October, we began to talk, to confide, to trust each other with the machinations of our minds and our sentiments.

We'd been married for 28 years and had started off with such a flurry. In fact, long before the matrimonial bans were read we'd spent years, decades, centuries, speaking, questioning, jousting and joshing. We'd learned each other's deepest feelings. We'd prised open the secret compartments of each other's souls, to learn whatever there was to be learned about this new and exciting person. This soul mate who'd entered our life and left our head spinning, our heart racing and our stomach churning, with that sense of awe which only those newly in love can know.

Out of this exquisite communion of our hearts a bond so strong and true had been forged that it had remained intact for all these years.

But now, without the constant buffing and polishing of our heartfelt feelings being articulated, the tarnish was there. In some insidious way it had evaded our warning systems and crept in under cover of complacency to dull the shine of our togetherness.

So few people appear to have the gift with which we have been blessed. So many have said they wished their love to be like ours. Yet, for all that those who have seen us as doyens of a love untarnished, there was a real and growing danger. Not that it was life threatening, but merely love threatening. Maybe not even that, but we had reached that stage in our life together when the temptation is to drift into a rippleless relationship. A steady snooze of spending time together, neither experiencing the exhilarating highs, nor the devastating lows that passion often demands as payment.

How we started this renewal was hesitantly. How else does one peel away the apprehensions developed over years of hiding certain inner feelings? Feelings of fear, of hurt, of frustration and failed expectations.

How hard is it to rectify those hours of irritation caused by seeing one's own faults occasionally mirrored in one's partner?

How brave must one be to confess finally that all those dreaming of the house on the hill, the holidays in Tuscany, the fine clothes and fancy living are in danger of slipping away, unattained and eventually unattainable?

How honest does one need to be to start again, to confess, to come clean, to broach brooding subjects that have been gathering dust on the shelves of our respective minds?

As difficult all that was for us, we somehow managed. Some issues came out snarling – sentiments hidden deep and dank, hissing as they reached the surface. Others were stuttered, semi-formed, half sentences that emerged little by little as our minds grappled with the task of expressing that which hurt to talk about. Some were things a little shameful, some sentimental, or seemingly silly, but nonetheless important to air.

It was…yes, it was fresh air breezing on our feelings. And as these feelings flowed, so too, did our passion for each other, for honesty between us, for that faith we needed, and will always need, to confide in each other.

Bent Thumb Thinking

To share, to help to shape, to support and strengthen.

We spoke, as we walked through that Spring-touched park in the morning, about the night before and the day ahead. We spoke as we dressed and breakfasted, about the future and what we dared to dream that it might hold for us. We spoke as we lay in bed at night, nestled together, two souls searching for unity, of our feelings for each other, of how we used to feel in those early days of studentship, secretly praying that he was the one, that she would have reciprocal feelings, that we could become us. We spoke of our joy and of our anguish.

We spoke and we spoke and we spoke.

And in all of those words were woven our love and our passion for what we had come to rediscover in each other and in ourselves. We cared for each other. We loved each other. And more important than either of those, we trusted each other.

As the pigeon trusts the air beneath her wings and the forces of flight to lift her above the ground and away from the dangers down there, we had faith in our love. Implicitly. Eternally. Unquestioningly.

We were again in flight together, our wings beating in harmony and our hearts again beating as one.

 "Well written and such good advice.."
— **Therese Religa**

27

A Job Interview That Started A Beautiful Relationship

Job interviews are all different. I've had formal ones, informal ones, even hilarious ones. Like most people, I've also had successful ones and a lot more that ended up going nowhere.

One factor that has been consistent, however, is that I've gone into every interview with a certain degree of apprehension.

It's quite a normal emotional state, because I have always started with an expectation that I'd be successful. This has nothing to do with arrogance or over-confidence, but without that positive outlook it would hardly be worth fronting up, would it?

But this interview was different – in every way.

My wife and son had decided that I should have a new dog. Ten years after my previous dog died, they believed it was time to renew my lifelong love for the animal species that, to me, makes the most loyal, forgiving and loving companion.

I like cats, but I love dogs. Perhaps it's because I see more of myself in the average dog than the average cat. Feed me, give me cuddles and I'm your friend. You don't even need to talk to me. No complications, no deep analysis, no hidden agendas. Simple, naïve, guileless. That's us – dogs and yours truly.

Cats are far more demanding in their relationships. Theirs is an affection you have to earn. It's conditional love. A dog will never leave you – a cat that finds better food a few doors down the road will go without a goodbye.

There was one complicating factor in the choice of dog I could have. My medical condition meant I was not steady on my feet and could easily be knocked over.

A puppy was out of the question. Training a young dog was not an option either. In fact, any dog that might behave in a boisterous manner was struck off the list.

My medical specialist mentioned that reclassified guide dogs were occasionally available for purchase, and encouraged us to explore that avenue.

So my name went down on the waiting list. And I waited. Forms arrived in the mail with a questionnaire that was extensive, to say the least. Where, what, who, how – all the questions were about the dog, with some interest shown in why we had applied for one of their dogs.

Months went by, so we began visiting dog shelters to find a suitable companion. But in the midst of this process I received a phone call.

"Are you still interested in a reclassified guide dog?

The answer was yes.

"There might be a suitable dog becoming available next week. I just wanted to check that you're still…"

"Oh yes!" I reassured her.

The next week came and went, then a month. We were in limbo regarding what to do. This was to be my birthday present, although nine months had elapsed since receiving a card explaining that the gift itself would be delivered later.

I received a second call, this time saying that the previous dog would not have been suitable, but there was one now.

"If you could come to the Guide Dogs facilities on Wednesday, at ten o'clock, the dog will interview you."

"Interview me?"

"Yes. You see, it's very important to establish your compatibility. The dog will know straight away. And we need to be sure your energy levels work well together."

This made me think. It sounded all upside down. Surely the human gets to choose? Not the dog!

But it also made me remember the stories of people buying puppies for Christmas, but by the end of January the fun of having a little furry animal bouncing around the house had been outweighed by the burden of feeding, walking and having to clean up the inevitable doggie doo. Poor dog!

That I was being interviewed now made sense. Of course it was not just the dog doing the investigation, because I'd been questioned twice, and had to submit a resume of sorts, before even making it to the meeting.

We arrived. I was not wearing my best suit and tie. It wasn't that kind of interview. But we did go up to a desk and state who we were and what our business was.

"Take a seat. The dog is on its way from Moonee Ponds. He'll be here soon."

Ah ha! A male dog. It was the only information we had.

We waited. A man came in with a dog on a lead. He handed the lead to the staff member who'd welcomed us. She smiled at us and, with a slight head movement, indicated that this was the interviewer.

"Wesley, this is Graham," she explained to a tall, slim, very smiley young Labrador who was described in his registration papers as yellow, although his coat was more the colour of a polar bear.

Wesley was led to where I was sitting. Very politely, and with no fuss or flurry, he looked at me and had a smell.

I'm told that dogs are very perceptive, measuring us by smell, posture, facial expression and by the energy field we transmit.

The interview was in progress. I stuck out my hand toward Wesley's nose. A wet response was also a good one. I was given the lead and walked around the reception room.

We went through the gardens, played a bit, and then I was asked to lead Wesley in a formal way, using the commands he'd been trained to respond to. It went well.

On returning to the reception the lady gave us her evaluation of the 'interview'.

"He was happy with you pretty much straight away. So that's good. And he came back to you in the playground when you called. So that was also good. And I think his energy level and yours are just about perfect for each other. So, if you're happy he can go home with you today."

Talk about a dream job – this was it. Wesley was fully trained, amazingly obedient, and had been bred for a gentle temperament.

The only problem we've had with him has been with water. Trained he is, but it seems you can't train the love of swimming out of a Lab. And he's not fussy about the water he jumps into.

At first sight Wesley and I were best friends, and he's right up there as one of the best birthday presents ever. Just quietly, I was warned that he was my birthday present for several birthdays to come. That was three birthdays ago.

I'm happy with that. Our relationship is excellent. We respect each other. We have fun together. We talk, although I do the talking and he listens. We don't live in each other's pockets.

And that's the way it should be between a dad and his boy. I'm his dad and my wife is mum. The only confused person in the family is my son. He can't quite come to terms with the idea that, if I'm Wesley's dad, then Wesley's his... BROTHER!?!?

 "What a lovely story, Graham. It made me feel rather teary. A man and his dog – you cannot say more."

– Marie Mander

28

A Grandson's Most Ingenious Excuse Ever

All grandparents are biased. It stands to reason. A grandchild is a direct result of your own existence, and represents a chance to boast and bigmouth with no reason whatsoever to feel ashamed or embarrassed.

After all, you played a part in creating them, and genetically you can claim to be why they are as smart or sporty or just generally wonderful as they are. Conversely, anything they do wrong almost certainly comes from a different part of their family tree.

It follows, therefore, that when I was summoned to oversee the punishment metered out on my grandson who'd refused to go to school, I felt no sense that he was letting down the family – not my side, anyway. But I did claim what followed during this time, because it was wonderfully inventive, daring and way beyond his years.

I arrived at the home of the offending child at around ten, to find a despairing mother and her defiant son.

He'd been confined to his bedroom with instructions that the only reason for leaving it was a need for the toilet, or if the house was burning down. He was to read, do schoolwork and not watch anything on a screen. No toys were allowed, either.

I said hello and explained to him that I'd be sitting in the lounge doing my work. Daughter disappeared to work and silence filled the house.

An hour went by, then two, when a movement caught my eye. It was James, padding down the passage like a shadow.

"Where are you going?" I asked, assuming I knew the answer.

"To the toilet," he replied. I nodded, because this is what I'd assumed.

"OK."

He proceeded and I went back to work on my laptop. Some time went by before I realised he'd not returned. I got up and walked into the kitchen, which was the way to the toilet. James was standing at the partly open back door, staring out. Wistfully.

"What are you doing?" I enquired.

"I need to go outside, Pa." (That's what he calls me – short for Grandpa.)

"Why's that?"

"Well," he explained in a very sombre and serious tone, "everyone knows that humans need ten minutes of sun every day…for Vitamin D…and I need mine."

"What? You sneaky little…You're trying to convince me that by not letting you out, I'll be responsible for damaging your health?" I didn't say these things, but I did think them with a wide, but invisible grin on my face.

He looked up at me, carefully calculating the effect of his logic on another human, who surely must know the simple scientific fact about this health requirement.

I looked back at him with great admiration. He'd learned something at school and was using it – for more than the health benefits.

I also almost picked him up and hugged him, thinking what a smart grandson I'd produced. Who else could possibly have a six-year-old quoting medical science to an adult with the intention of getting off his punishment?

He came within a whisker of being allowed to take ten minutes outside in the sun. But then my sense of responsibility slapped me on the back of the head.

"Unfortunately, James, your mum has instructed you and me that you're to stay in your room until she comes home. So that's what it has to be. When she gets back you can discuss your Vitamin D situation with her."

He nodded, took a longing look at the back garden bathed in that essential sunlight, and walked back to his room. No look of unfairness, no sigh of sadness, was heard. He'd given it his best shot, but accepted that Pa was not about to overrule mum.

My claim that the ingenuity of his argument coming from my genetic gift to him, has been the source of some anguish for me. The reason is simply that I would never in my wildest imaginings have been able to come up with a story like that. It must just have been him.

29

Adult Immigration

This is a story about reading signs. I'm not talking about road signs, but signs that indicate whether or not to progress down a particular path.

Nine years after returning to South Africa from our first foray into life overseas, we were ready to try again. There were two contenders – the USA and Australia. America was Gaynor's choice, which is understandable considering she had spent a life-changing year in that country as an exchange student.

I, on the other hand, had a preference for Australia. My reasons were both simple and simplistic. Australians play the sports I'd grown up with, they live a predominantly outdoor life, which I'm used to. And the beer, in my opinion, is better. All important considerations.

There was also a cultural issue that steered me in the direction of the Antipodean choice.

Working in Canada, as a writer, I'd faced the reality that North America was way more into Disney than it was into Grimm's fairy tales. Mickey Mouse meant more to people there than Hansel and Gretel or Rumplestiltskin. This might sound insignificant, but writing is so much about idioms and culture, and I'd found out that my background was set in British and European culture, rather than new world.

We flew off to Sydney, ostensibly for a holiday. But I had compiled a small portfolio of my work to show to interested parties in this foreign place.

The aeroplane is where we had the first sign, although at the time it was not obvious.

Early on Saturday morning, still about two hours out of Sydney, we discovered our dentist and his wife were on the flight. He had mysteriously disappeared about three years previously and now we knew where he had gone.

"It's so nice to see you again," he said. "Are you also living in Australia now?"

We explained that we were on our first visit.

"Where are you staying while you're in Sydney?" he asked.

Gaynor and I looked at each other somewhat bashfully and I replied.

"We haven't really organised accommodation yet. We'll do it when we get there, because we don't know how long we're going to be there."

The dentist instantly began a promotion of the hotel we should book into. Australians will all know that the details suggest a very expensive place, but we were none the wiser. It's a very exclusive suburb.

"It's a boutique hotel in Double Bay," he explained. "It's run by a Dutch fellow and his wife. And he loves South Africans. In fact, he even flies a South African flag out the front".

We noted this and took down all the details. Having agreed that this was a good idea and sat down for the final part of the flight. It was a great start and a positive sign.

Having landed we went through the normal procedures early on that Saturday morning. We filled in forms, collected luggage and lined up to go through Customs and Immigration.

This Immigration Officer was very different to the one I had encountered ten years before. He looked at our passports and looked at us to confirm we were the same people. Then he said something I will never forget

"Gaynor! Lovely name. I had a girlfriend once call Gaynor. Lovely girl." He smiled and pushed the passport towards us. "Have a lovely time in Australia."

It was a very different introduction to a new country. Quite different from anything we had experienced before or since.

Off we went, pulling our suitcases, jumped in a taxi and headed for Double Bay. (Locals refer to it as 'Double Pay' because of how expensive it is.)

Believe it or not this hotel was extremely reasonable and the owner amazingly friendly. We checked in and spent the weekend taking trains, buses and walks around this beautiful city called Sydney, soaking up the atmosphere of the easy-going nature of Australia.

On the Monday I checked into a specialist advertising placement agency and was immediately plugged into the owner who lived and worked in Melbourne.

We also caught up with a few people we knew in Sydney, one of whom was a copywriter like me. We'd worked in the same ad agency in Cape Town. When he heard I was going to a job interview in Melbourne, he warned me.

"Whatever they offer you, don't take it. That town dies at nine each night. And the weather…"

The next thing we did was to follow the advice of an Aussie friend of mine in South Africa. He had a very fancy name but came from a very small town call Yackandanda. Royston had advised me not to hire a car, but rather to buy one on the understanding that the dealer would take it back after three weeks for an agreed price.

It made sense to me, so I asked the Dutch hotelier if he could direct me to a car dealer. He thought for a moment and he gave us directions. It was that close by that Gaynor and I set out on foot immediately. Five kilometres later I saw the first sign of the car dealership, but my heart sank. It was a familiar three pointed star and I didn't have that kind of money.

We walked in and asked for the man we'd been instructed to speak to. He proceeded to enquire about what model of Mercedes Benz we were interested in.

"I think there's been a misunderstanding," I explained. "I'm just looking for a cheap used car for our three week holiday in Australia."

The sales person rubbed his chin and proceeded to speak in a dialect of English I couldn't follow. It included lots of "no worries" and "yeah mate". These were terms I wasn't familiar with.

"Do you know where I could find something like that?" I asked.

He said something I didn't understand, then picked up the phone and dialled. The conversation that ensued was like listening to a foreign language. Our ears hadn't become accustomed to the Aussie accent and this man had a strong one. An hour later I'd bought a ten-year-old Valiant, in perfect condition, for $1,000. We'd agreed that in three weeks' time he would take it back and refund $850.

Come to think of it, there was no paperwork and no third party insurance. A handshake did the trick.

We travelled all the way to Brisbane and back in the next ten days stopping at every interesting place along the way. One of these was Willow Tree, a hamlet of five or six houses, a grain silo next to the railway line, and a store.

Gaynor was suffering from chapped lips, so she wanted some lip ointment. I stopped and she went in. After what seemed way too long to make a simple purchase, she climbed into the car and told me what had happened.

"I couldn't find the lip ice. I went down both aisles – twice. The man asked me what I was looking for, and when I told him, he said: 'Ice? For your lips?' I told him I had chapped lips and he said: 'You want lip balm, luv. Lip BALM!'"

"He showed me where it was and then asked me where I was from. When I told him we're from South Africa he nearly fell over. Then he said: 'I thought only pygmies lived there. You know, little short, dark fellas.'"

We'll always remember Willow Tree.

On returning to Sydney, the fairy godmother of advertising in Melbourne explained that she had one more interview for me, this one was not in Sydney.

"These people would like to fly you down for some interviews. They're happy to fly your wife down as well if she'd like to."

"Let me ask her."

I held my hand over the phone and explained to Gaynor. She declined instantly.

"OK," I said. "If I go on my own and what I see, you're happy for me to decide?"

"I'll come with you," was the immediate response.

We flew to Melbourne that Friday morning. It was a wet August day. There was a mist in the air and a gentleness in the atmosphere. We looked at each other in the cab on the way to our appointment and smiled.

"It's just like Cape Town…without the mountain." We said this in unison.

Without going into detail, the interview went well, that evening was a riot, and we'd been invited to spend the weekend in Melbourne at the expense of the ad agency. These were all good signs. But they were not the deciders.

Call me shallow if you will, but what clinched the deal was on Saturday afternoon. We'd spent all day walking through the botanical gardens, into the city and through the arcades.

We loved what we'd seen, but were now back in our hotel room looking over Albert Park, with the lake across the road. We were starving.

Gaynor decided to take a shower, while I organised some room service. I ordered two hamburgers with the lot, and two beers and one lemonade. Gaynor liked a shandy, but every beer drinker will know that using part of your beer for somebody else's shandy means you don't have a whole beer for yourself. That's why I ordered two.

Ten minutes later there was a knock on the door and the order arrived. I signed and stared. These were two of the biggest hamburgers I'd ever seen, and the beers were not the normal 375ml cans. They were bloke sized 500ml cans.

I was in heaven. When Gaynor came out of the shower I made it plain what I intended to do with regard to our future.

"This is where we're going to live. I love this city and I love all this." I pointed at the hamburgers and the beer cans with a big beam on my face.

There was one more sign that sealed the deal. That was, depending on whether I was offered the job.

A few days later we were in Sydney International Airport, heading back home. We checked in our luggage, filled in the appropriate forms and, when our flight was called, proceeded through Immigration. We were summoned, walked forward, and Gaynor handed over our passports. The officer picked them up.

"Ah, Gaynor! I saw you coming in a few weeks ago. I wouldn't forget that name. Hope you've had a wonderful time in our country."

That was it. We knew this was the country for us. Four months later we'd had our interview with Australian Immigration and received our visas. It just remained for us to sell our house, pack up our belongings and head for our new home.

We arrived very appropriately on a weekend in late January, which has a special significance for us. It was Australia Day when we touched down in our new home.

30

The Worst Kind Of Bully

For many young boys sport and education are diametrically opposed. Time in the classroom, for those boys, is time wasted. It could be much better spent on the sports ground, honing their kicking, catching or throwing.

That isn't how I started out, but it is how I ended up, as a schoolboy. I came first in my first year, but by the time I'd reached the end of primary school, my position had slid to rather near the bottom of the class.

The catalyst for change was bullying.

Most children experience some form of bullying. On most of these occasions the bully is a peer – somebody a similar age in the circle of friends or acquaintances. In my case it was neither of these. It was a teacher. As a nine-year-old I was subjected on a weekly basis to ridicule by the class teacher.

What Mr Osborne would do was call me out, stand me on the teacher's plinth, and then completely ignore me. What he did instead was speak to the rest of the class of boys – about me.

"You see this boy"? He would say, looking at the class but pointing at me.

"This boy is a hopeless case. He doesn't work hard in class. He sits and looks out the window. Dreaming. And where will that get him. I'll tell you. For a start, he'll be uneducated. And because of that, he won't amount to anything. This boy will end up being a 'no good'. He'll join one of those gangs of young thugs that get up to bad things. The next step from there – he'll probably end up a criminal and eventually find himself in jail."

Today that kind of treatment from a teacher would not be tolerated, but at the time there was nothing anyone could do about it.

I have no idea what the rest of the class thought when these tirades were going on, but I do know how I felt. Small, weak, stupid, powerless. A failure.

I was already a quiet child. Through this treatment I became silent, retreating into my own world. Each time this happened my self-esteem declined a little further. The way I imagined the other boys viewed me was the worst part. Surely they believed what the teacher said. He was the teacher, after all. And teachers know everything – certainly in the mind of a nine-year-old.

Academically my world declined. So did my social and sporting life. I was trapped in this bubble of low expectation about everything. I'd bought the lies Mr. Osborne had spoken about me.

The way out was drastic for me at that time.

Three years after my 'annus horribilus' (horrible year), and now struggling in class, on the sports field and even at home, my father suggested a change of school.

Like most people who are unsure of themselves, I was averse to change. After much gentle persuasion about the benefits of the move, I reluctantly and very timidly headed off to boarding school at the age of thirteen.

This is where redemption happened. Gradually. Although I'd been cut loose from the bully geographically, his words travelled with me. In my head and in my heart.

At the start of the first term, on the tuck shop notice board, was a section for each of the many sports available. I liked cricket and wanted to participate. In the 'Cricket' section was a sheet with columns for your name, previous school and the team played in the previous year.

The first two columns were easy, but the third column was awkward. Having been convinced I was useless, the team I'd played for was the Under 13E's. Nothing to boast about.

A week later cricket trials were held to sort out the talented from the less able. By the end of those proceedings I managed to elevate myself to the Under 14A's and B's.

I couldn't believe it. The school either had unbelievably low standards, or I was not nearly as bad as I'd thought.

At the end of that term similar lists went up. This time I was focussed on rugby. The same three columns were filled out with the exact same details, including Under 13E as my previous team. At the end of the trials I had managed to run, tackle and pass my way into the Under 14A's.

Now I was convinced. This new school had standards way below my expectations. You see, I'd imagined that most of the boys would be way better than me, but they weren't. I'm not saying I was outstanding, but at least I wasn't well below average. And that was my real expectation.

Another interesting thing started to happen in parallel with this.

Because nobody at this new school knew of my inadequacies, the labels my bully had pinned on me a few years previously, started to fade. As my sporting achievements progressed, so did my recovery from a low self-worth.

This is only my story, and I understand that bullying should never be condonable. However, the choice I made as a nine-year-old, which was to buy what the teacher said about me, proved to be a mistake. As I moved away from what he said, in time and geography, I realised that they were only his opinion, and I had the choice of accepting or rejecting them.

This is why sport has been so important in my life. As I was growing up it taught me such valuable lessons, like perseverance, perspective and believing in myself. It was to some extent my salvation.

Bullying is rife in our society. Sadly, it doesn't end necessarily when we grow up.

As an adult a cruel and relentless new bully became a part of my life in two thousand and nine. In December of that year I was diagnosed with Motor Neuron Disease (ALS in the USA).

Since then every day it has confronted me, and I have had to confront it. Luckily, through those lessons I learnt as a schoolboy, I know that attitude is the greatest weapon against bullying.

Bullies are often cowards, and they almost always use fear as their biggest weapon. Doubt is the end product of fear, and that leads to a life lived with the handbrake on.

I heard it said that "FEAR" stands for "False Evidence Appearing Real", and have used this as a mantra of sorts. Not that I have ever disbelieved what the medical people in my current situation have said to me, but I've chosen to examine their prognoses closely and choose my attitude towards what they say.

Not having had any medical training, my examination hinges on a single tenet:

"Everything they say to me is based on worst case scenario, so that I don't get my hopes up too far. Everything I say to myself should be based on best case scenario, because that's how I keep my hopes (and my mental health) up."

There's an exciting new development in neural science that suggests how our thinking affects our physical brain, which in turn affects our physical body. By "renewing our mind" through harnessing how we allow ourself to think, we can influence our health.

Believe that or not. It's your choice, just like it is mine.

The fact that a teacher chose to make a mockery of me as a young boy has left no bitterness or malice. But what it has left, through the bumps and bruises of the sporting arena, is that I choose how I will respond to anything said about me. By anyone! Especially a bully. Even MND.

So anyone who considers sport simply to be a mindless exercise in chasing a piece of leather or running and swimming faster, or trying to beat the next person, fails to understand that the real enemy for most of us lives within. Sport is a great teacher of how to overcome this assumption, often placed there by our own self-doubt.

Postscript

In the past few years I've been asked by a number of people what I put my longer than normal survival as a Motor Neuron Disease sufferer down to. Do I have any idea why I've managed to beat the average, which is twenty-seven months?

In all honesty, the best answer I can come up with sounds quite self-serving, because I simply say it's a sense of purpose.

This may appear to suggest that I believe those who don't survive as long as I have, just don't have this. Please be assured. This is not my view. Far from it.

Something that has been a great asset to me in the last few years is a narrative that answers an age old query. It may mean nothing to you, but this book is filled with anecdotes about the stepping stones that have brought me from there to here. For that reason only I want to share this one.

What Am I Doing Here?

All of us, especially when we're facing a challenge, are inclined to go through the anguish of trying to figure out the answer to the question that has tormented humans for millennia.

In a conversation before commencing a bible study, the topic came up that every one of us, at some stage grapples with.

What am I doing here? Or more specifically, what is my purpose in life?

My conclusion came to me, sitting on a park bench in the weak winter sun, watching my best friend, Wesley, snuffling around in the scrub, smelling smells only dogs can understand.

Earlier that morning I'd been to a men's group meeting, where four hardy souls gathered fortnightly to discuss a passage of scripture.

The reading was something Jesus said to his disciples:

"I am the vine; you are the branches. If a man remains in me and I in him, he will bear much fruit; apart from me you can do nothing."

We all understood that this was something each one of them would have resonated with. After all, in those days everyone had a closeness to agriculture that most people in our cities don't have today.

And as I sat, with the sun gently warming me, I meditated on the morning's scripture.

In humility and in no way trying to improve on the metaphor of the vine Jesus uses to teach us, here's a picture that was painted in my mind.

It's a modern metaphor which made my personal answer to that age old question a little easier. Like most metaphors it does break down at a certain point, but nevertheless it may illuminate a pathway for contemplations on a higher level.

Consider this:

I am like a solar panel.

To be the best I can be I am focussed towards the sun. I absorb and take my energy from that source – the source of all power. The power I absorb is then relayed to the grid, providing power to the greater community, for the greater good.

If I do that, then I'm fulfilling the purpose for which my creator made me. I am a productive solar panel, and when the sun goes down I can rest happily. Of course, I don't have to, but I choose to, in recognition of what that creator gives me.

Many people are like this, plugged in, productive solar panels. But many more are not. Many are neither plugged in nor producing as they were designed to do.

The reason is so simple to understand in this metaphorical example. Imagine. If I turn my focus away from the sun, then my productivity is diminished. If I am in shadow or darkness, my productivity declines even further, receding eventually into non-existence.

What if I'm unplugged – disconnected from the other panels and the grid? In that case I might be doing all the right things but for no worthwhile purpose.

I might even choose to say: "I don't need to proclaim my belief in the sun, or work specifically for the grid. I'm not doing anyone any harm. I'm basically a good, clean living little solar panel."

If I say that, then I'm one of the many solar panels that remain, in a sense, still wrapped up in our original bubble wrap and box, doing nothing wrong, if we are looking at the small picture of life. But viewing the bigger picture, these panels are wasting the very purpose for which they were created.

The purpose of being a solar panel is simple:

Focus on the source of all power and use it to bring light and warmth to the nations.

Or as Jesus put it: **Love the Lord your God with all your soul and with all your might. And love your neighbour as yourself.**

Amen.

MOTOR NEURONE DISEASE ASSOCIATION OF VICTORIA INC.
Registered Association No. A7518
ABN 44 113 484 160
265 Canterbury Road (PO Box 23)
Canterbury 3126
Australia
Tel: + 61 3 9830 2122
Fax: + 61 3 9830 2228
Email: info@mnd.asn.au

Motor Neurone Disease Association of Victoria was established in 1981 by a group of families impacted by MND. Their mission then, as it remains today, is to provide and promote the best possible care and support to people living with MND.

Every day someone in Victoria living with MND is facing a new challenge as their disease progresses. Thankfully, the Association's MND Advisor service is there with them to help navigate the complex health and funding options. In addition, MND Victoria's equipment service provides equipment at no cost to the person with MND and helps them remain connected with their family, friends and the wider community and maintains safety in and out of home for family, friends and paid carers. Last year MND Victoria provided 1,644 pieces of equipment to families throughout Victoria.

To ensure we can continue to deliver care and support services to people with MND the Association needs to raise 70% of its funding, or over $3 million, every year. We are very grateful to Graham and Gaynor Crossan for choosing to donate $1 to MND Victoria for every copy of *Bent Thumb Thinking* sold.

Each year in Australia more than 2,000 people have MND, and every day two people are diagnosed with MND and two people die from the disease. In 2016/17 financial year, MND Victoria supported 574 Victorians living with MND. For more information:

Phone: 1-800 806 632
Email: info@mnd.asn.au
Web: www.mnd.asn.au
Facebook: https://www.facebook.com/MNDVic/
Instagram: www.instagram.com/mnd_vic/

Acknowledgements

In this modern world, where there is so much talk of conflict and dispute, I'm happy to acknowledge that there are plenty of wonderful people. To prove my point I will even go so far as to name a few.

Without these people in my life, and actively participating in it, you would not be reading this book. To each one of them I say a huge 'thank you'.

For starters, my immediate family, past and present: these stories are, for the most part, about my time with you.

In particular, Gaynor, who has lived with a storyteller for almost half a century, thanks for enduring the wild rides and the precarious paths you've travelled because of me. Thanks also for providing me with two wonderful children, Simon and Ande, who have played integral parts in many of my stories.

Cameron and James were the driving forces in the road trip that led to my emergence as a storyteller. Well driven. We got there and back in safety.

The other driving forces are friends I hadn't seen for thirty years, who suddenly were back in my life in a big way, convincing me to start the blog, then encouraging me and guiding me, even into print. Walter Dobrowolski and Victor Kazan, thank you. And Andrew Dobrowolski, your camera work was invaluable.

There is a large collection of other people who have

played their parts. Maryann Cain, Debbie White, Bryan and Dawn Patterson, Helen MacGregor, Brenda Addie, and the wonderful people at Busybird Publishing, please accept my gratitude.

Everyone who pledged in the crowdfunding, and those who wished us well in the endeavour, I am indebted to each one of you. You provided the fuel and the fanfare to get us going.

And then there are all the people who have written encouraging comments, or simply clicked 'like' on Bent Thumb Thinking. To you I say, keep up the good work. Every one of us needs all the encouragement we can get. So keep spreading the love.

Supporters of BTT

Alexandra Dobrowolski
Alice McGhee
Andrea Drake
Anne Kelly
Antonia Jenny Rumngevur
Astrid Browne
Beverley Simpson
Bruce Duperouzel
Bryan Patterson
Burke Bond Partners
Busybird Publishing
Cain Family
Caroline Dew
Cathy Vining
Cathy Yates
Cheryl Funston
Chris MacDonald
Crossan/Edgar Family
Debbie White
Doug Lumley
Edwards/Morris Family
Elizabeth Edgar
Fiona Edgar
Gary Tennant
Gillian Lechte
Janita Friend
Jenn Roberts
Jo Gilbert
Karen Christensen
Karl Siegling
Kate Croucher
Kevin Purcell
Lauren Yuen
Lee Thorn
Liesl Williams
Liz Douglas
Liza Pook
Marie Mander
Marika Cosmas
Mark Featherby
Mary Saunderson
Mary Tunnell-Jones
Mel Barassi
Melissa Butler
Melissa Martin
Mike & Sally Davies
Natalie Raccosta
Rina Stefani
Rosie Gibb
Sandra Cavallo
Sarah Mander
Scott Ian Gordon
Selwyn Blackstone
Statewide Assets Pty Ltd
Sue & John Watson
Suzi Harris
Terry Johal
Tracey Foster
Trish & Ross Baldwin
Trudi McGrath
Wendy Cheesman
Winther/Scrivener Family
Yassamin Rakers-Rahimi
Yukiko Goh
Yvonne Johnson

www.ingramcontent.com/pod-product-compliance
Lightning Source LLC
Chambersburg PA
CBHW031112080526
44587CB00011B/946